reckless ABANDON

**Charisma®
HOUSE**

LARRY TOMCZAK

author of quarter-million bestseller *Clap Your Hands*

RECKLESS ABANDON by Larry Tomczak
Published by Charisma House
A part of Strang Communications Company
600 Rinehart Road
Lake Mary, Florida 32746
www.charismahouse.com

Unless otherwise noted, all Scripture quotations are from the Holy
Bible, New International Version. Copyright © 1973, 1978, 1984,
International Bible Society. Used by permission.

Scripture quotations marked KJV are from the King James Version
of the Bible.

Scripture quotations marked NAS are from the New American
Standard Bible. Copyright © 1960, 1962, 1963, 1968, 1971, 1972,
1973, 1975, 1977 by the Lockman Foundation.
Used by permission. (www.Lockman.org)

Scripture quotations marked NKJV are from the New King James
Version of the Bible. Copyright © 1979, 1980, 1982 by Thomas
Nelson, Inc., publishers. Used by permission.

Scripture quotations marked NRSV are from the New Revised
Standard Version of the Bible. Copyright © 1989 by the Division
of Christian Education of the National Council of the Churches of
Christ in the USA. Used by permission.

Scripture quotations marked RSV are from the Revised Standard
Version of the Bible. Copyright © 1946, 1952, 1971 by the
Division of Christian Education of the National Council of the
Churches of Christ in the USA.
Used by permission.

Cover design by Rachel Campbell

Library of Congress Catalog Card Number: 2002104310
International Standard Book Number: 0-88419-876-6

01 02 03 04   87654321
Printed in the United States of America

This book is dedicated to my wife, Doris, my four children and the following pioneers whom I count as friends and who have impacted my life. I know there are multitudes more. May the circle be ever expanding. Special thanks goes to Michael Klassens, an excellent editor, for his skillful assistance in shaping the contents to its finalized state.

Che Ahn
Francis Anfuso
Dick Benjamin
Mike Brown
Mike Bickle
Mike Coleman
Lindell Cooley
Paul Cain
Gerald Coates
Richard Crisco
Frank Damazio
Lou Engle
Rob "Donut Man" Evans
Bill Galbraith
Melody Green
Joe & Ann Grefenstette
Bill Greig III
Tom Hess
Benny Hinn
Eric Holmberg
Steve Hill
Dick Iverson
Bryn Jones
Rick Joyner
John Kilpatrick

Bob Legg
Ron Luce
Don Milan Jr.
Bill McCartney
Lattie McDonough
Bob Mumford
Derek Prince
Winkie Pratney
Bart Pierce
Pat Robertson
Kenny Roberts
Charles Simpson
Stephen Strang
Charles & Dotty Schmitt
Wendel Smith
Tommy Tenney
David Van Cronkite
Terry Virgo
Peter Wagner
Bob Weiner
John Wimber
The leadership team at
    Christ the King Church
    of Atlanta

I also want to honor Billy Graham who has been a role model to me since I began in ministry and is a true pioneer within the body of Christ worldwide.

Finally, and primarily, I want to offer a fresh dedication of my life and ministry to the One who saved me and set me free to fulfill my destiny in life—my Lord and Savior, Jesus Christ.

> Therefore, since we are surrounded by such a great cloud of witnesses, let us throw off everything that hinders and the sin that so easily entangles, and let us run with perseverance the race marked out for us. Let us fix our eyes on Jesus, the [pioneer] and perfecter of our faith, who for the joy set before him endured the cross, scorning its shame, and sat down at the right hand of the throne of God.
> —HEBREWS 12:1–2

Contents

The Kingdom of God is not going to advance by our churches becoming filled with people but by people in our churches becoming filled with God.

—HOWARD SPRING
CHRISTIAN AUTHOR AND TEACHER

Don't worry about how to gather a crowd. Go out, catch fire, and people will come to watch you burn!

—JOHN WESLEY
18TH-CENTURY APOSTLE AND HISTORY MAKER

The doom of a nation can only be averted by a storm of glowing passion.

—ADOLPH HITLER
POTENTIAL PREACHER WHOSE
DESTINY WAS TRAGICALLY DIVERTED

Do not go where there is a path. Instead, go where others haven't gone, and leave a trail.

—RALPH W. EMERSON
1800S POET

I have come to bring fire on the earth, and how I wish it were already kindled!

—JESUS CHRIST
SON OF GOD AND SAVIOR
OF THE WORLD (LUKE 12:49)

A New Day Dawning for Christianity— Twenty Earmarks

Y ou and I are witnessing a rapidly approaching moment in time when forces will converge, producing cataclysmic change. With the threat of terrorism already at North America's doorstep, life as we knew it in the twentieth century no longer exists. Reluctantly, we have been dragged into the insecure and threatened environment that the nations of two-thirds of our world have experienced for decades— even centuries.

These changes, however, didn't begin with the terrorist attacks on the Pentagon and World Trade Center. They began when the heart of this nation turned away from God. Here is a snapshot of what is happening *today* in our country:

> ➢ Seven thousand couples will divorce, affecting the lives of over ten thousand children.

[handwritten top margin: "The stinging Emptyness it Feels Inside!" → "The heart! / the human / dead spirit) / the essence of man"]

R e c k l e s s   A b a n d o n

[handwritten left margin: "2" / "RU-486" / "Home Abortion kit"]

- One in five adults will carry a sexually transmitted disease.

- More then four thousand babies will be murdered. Abortion has never been easier to obtain than now when we've legalized RU-486—the home abortion kit—and reaffirmed the legality of partial-birth abortion.

- Through the media many of our children will be poisoned by increasingly explicit and perverted sex, violence, profanity and blasphemy. One-half of all Internet subscribers will engage in pornography, averaging ten hours per week per person.

- Homosexuality, lesbianism and other deviant lifestyles will be paraded and promoted on *mainstream* network television (non-cable stations) as normal behavior.

[handwritten left margin: "Key!"] Our culture cries out for an antidote to the stinging emptiness it feels inside, but many people in the church are afraid to risk defiling themselves. Instead we stand by idly with nothing to offer but empty platitudes of "Be warmed, and be filled."

While our nation unravels before our eyes, many fail to realize the gravity of what's going on around us. We're like the man on the street whom the pollster asked, "What seems to be a greater problem in our nation—ignorance or apathy?"

His response: "I don't know, and I don't care."

During this turbulent period of generational transition, we face two choices. We can either stick our heads in the sand and pretend that the storm around us doesn't exist, or we can tilt our spiritual ears to the wind of the Holy Spirit and "hear what the Spirit says to the churches" (Rev. 2:7).

I believe Jesus Christ is calling you and me to turn

[handwritten bottom margin: "Holy Spirit 'wind' long me to wher you want me to bear the fruit that will give the Father a Son glory & Honor!"]

NO RETREAT! TOTAL commitment to A CAUSE!
"The CAUSE OF Christ"

the tide of history. Before us lies the dawn of a new day for Christianity. →only for the Remnant?

Will you join me in this move of God?

THERE'S NO TURNING BACK

I am convinced we are living in a critical moment when God is imparting wisdom and passion into the spiritual DNA of His people—people who are dissatisfied with ignorance and apathy. But moving forward through these perilous times requires the determination of a pioneer rather than the self-assuredness of the settler.

When Julius Caesar crossed the Rubicon, he waited until the last of his troops crossed over the river, and then he issued the order: "Burn the bridge!"

After his fleet landed on Mexico's shores, Hernando Cortez, the great Spanish explorer, instructed his men to burn all their ships.

I believe God is giving us the same message: No retreat! We face a decisive moment when total commitment to a cause is required in order to succeed.

OUR IGNORANCE AND APATHY POINT TO OUR NEED FOR REVIVAL

The state of our schools—violence, drugs, immorality, illiteracy, rebellion and secularism—points to a need for revival.

The demise of our pop culture—music, films, television, the arts—points to a need for revival.

The condition of our families, churches and government points to a need for revival. Without revival, our

4   nation will inevitably fall apart from within, as it is already beginning to do.

God is awakening His church to the urgency of the hour and the potential for true revival—which is really just getting the church *back* to normal—in this extraordinary era.

The Great Wall of China is fifteen hundred miles long, so extensive that our astronauts were able to see it from the moon, and twenty-three centuries old. The wall was constructed to protect China's inhabitants from outside enemies, yet China still suffered invasions from without. Why did this happen? It happened because the watchmen and gatekeepers who guarded the wall compromised their responsibilities through bribery and moral corruption. China's greatest threat came from within! You and I are watchmen and gatekeepers on a great spiritual wall. May we learn from China's example to beware of threats from within as well as from without.

Every Christian carries the responsibility of being a gatekeeper and a watchman on the wall that surrounds the soul of our nation. Unless we reverse the slide into an abyss of moral decay, the moral and spiritual wall surrounding our nation will suffer the same fate as China's Great Wall. Our only hope is heaven-sent revival.

Paul sounded an alarm in the first century: "The hour has come for you to wake up from your slumber" (Rom. 13:11). My hope, twenty centuries later, is to follow in Paul's footsteps by sounding a wake-up call to you as you read this book.

Twenty Earmarks That Signal a   5
Fresh Move of God

Students of church history recognize the telltale signs that signal God is getting ready to intervene in a supernatural way among His people. These general signs include:

- A consecration to holiness
- A fresh commitment to worship and fervent prayer
- A passion for God's presence
- The pursuit of authentic New Testament Christianity

Just as He did two thousand years ago, God is about to "[turn] the world upside down" (Acts 17:6, NKJV). A spiritual revolution is underway. A new day is dawning for Christianity!

As I witness where God is already at work among His people, the twenty components listed below are evidence that we stand on the frontier of a new move of God:

1. Passion for Jesus and His manifest presence
2. A fresh expectancy that a genuine awakening is at hand
3. Awareness of the urgency of the hour and the gravity of the situation
4. Extraordinary prayer and newfound delight in Spirit-led fasting
5. A return to extravagant praise and worship as modeled in David's tabernacle
6. Holy living that springs from a love for Jesus rather than legalism

7. Hunger for more and more and more of God

8. A growing distaste for worldly enticements and distractions

9. Humility and brokenness amid a "nameless, faceless" generation of emerging leaders

10. Spirit-led cooperation and colaboring within the wider body of Christ

11. Intergenerational ministry—parents and youth together

12. The church arising as a countercultural community

13. Team ministry and relationship-oriented leadership

14. Lifestyle evangelism and world missions that are relational, natural and servant-based

15. The receptive embrace of the high calling of womanhood and women's involvement in ministry

16. Recovery of true supernatural ministry—gifts, signs and wonders—that stems from God's presence in our midst

17. Restoration of the Ephesians 4:11 gift ministries of apostle and prophet

18. A new breed of planted churches that model authentic New Testament Christianity

19. Church gatherings that reflect Spirit-borne creativity and spontaneity

20. Compassionate ministry to the needy—the poor, the widow, the orphan and the oppressed

All of the earmarks are still germinating below the soil of what most people can see. But in order for these seeds to sprout into a fruitful, palpable move of God, a paradigm shift must take place among the people of God. First-century Christianity impact comes when twenty-first-century Christians function as pioneers—not settlers. That's what this book is all about.

GOD CREATED US WITH ADVENTUROUS HEARTS

You and I were created with wild and adventurous hearts. We long for new experiences, the adrenaline rush that accompanies our unexpected discoveries and the promise of joys and blessings yet to be fulfilled. Yet our human nature yearns for security, comfort, stability and the status quo.

As Christians—especially when we are new Christians—our craving for new experiences is energized by our confident trust that we are in God's hands. He loves us, and we believe that He will protect us. This trust heightens our thirst for adventure. We're like the child standing at the top of the stairs with our daddy standing below, his arms outstretched, saying, *"C'mon, jump!* I'll catch you."* We jump because we know that our daddy will catch us—and the thrill is immeasurable.

And yet, as we "mature," we tend to risk less. Comfort and predictability become sacred. Why? In part, because a lifetime of disappointments and small failures breeds within us a subtle spirit of fear. Self-protection becomes the dominant theme in our lives, and we hold on to what we have lest someone take it all away. Our trust in God is slowly undermined by a trust in our own self-preservation, self-discipline, self-confidence and self-security. Does this mean our faith in God is gone? No. Inside still exists a wild and passionate heart after

God. But our spiritual senses become calloused by the bumps and bruises of everyday life.

A brief survey of the men and women of faith in God's Word quickly shows us that God doesn't call us to lives of safety and security. He calls us to walk by faith—not by sight (2 Cor. 5:7). Without faith it is impossible to please God (Heb. 11:6).

Through this book I hope to come alongside you and to awaken within you the desire to trust God more. Learn to leap off the top of the stairs into the strong arms of your loving, laughing heavenly Father. This book will help you to unleash the Spirit of God within you so He can have His will and His way in your life once again—without reservation and without fear. Stir up that pioneer spirit. Take *big* risks, because the rewards are even bigger!

I invite you to join me on the adventure of a lifetime! Ask God to give you a Spirit-led, reckless abandon to join the swelling ranks of spiritual pioneers arising in our day.

GOD HAS CALLED US TO FINISH THE RACE

If you've become discouraged or disillusioned, take hope. Your past is not the blueprint for your future.

The great pioneer Paul the Apostle once said, "I have fought the good fight, I have finished the race, I have kept the faith" (2 Tim. 4:7). There is a way for you to live your life so someday you will be able to echo his words—"I too have fought my good fight . . . finished my race . . . and kept the faith!" But, as Derek Prince reminds us, "There is no way to finish the race and keep the faith without fighting the fight."

Regardless of where you've been or what you've been through, it's time to fight the good fight and run the race until the race is finished.

In the 1968 Mexico City Olympics, a Tanzanian runner named John Steven Aquari emerged from the cold darkness. He entered at the far end of the stadium with excruciating pain hobbling his every step. One of his legs was bloody, bruised and bandaged due to a fall he had taken earlier in the race. An hour had already passed since the winner of the Olympic marathon had been declared. Few spectators remained, yet this lone runner continued his difficult task. As he crossed the finish line, the sparse crowd erupted in supportive applause. He finally finished the race.

Afterward a reporter inquired of the courageous runner why he had not withdrawn from the race when he knew he had no chance of winning. John Stephen seemed perplexed by the question. Finally he answered.

"My country did not send me to the Olympics to start the race. They sent me to finish."

Fellow pioneers, God has called us to do likewise with reckless abandon. To do anything less would mean falling short of God's adventurous plans for our lives. May we do our part not merely to perpetuate an inauthentic, anemic form of Christianity, but rather to portray the real thing for the honor of the real Jesus we so love. And in the end, may we hear our heavenly Father say, "Well done, good and faithful servant" (Matt. 25:21).

One

Tomorrow's Man

Larry Tomczak, you are tomorrow's man!"

Listening attentively to Gerald Coates address two thousand Christians in the sweltering Pasadena auditorium, I was startled that this animated speaker from England spontaneously heralded my name in the middle of his message.

Why would he interrupt his sermon to give me a little prophetic encouragement? I wondered.

"Larry Tomczak, you are tomorrow's man!" His statement punctuated the air a second time, this time even more emphatically. As quickly as he said it, he resumed his train of thought, leaving me to ponder his words. *Tomorrow's man ... tomorrow's man ... what did this mean? Why was I singled out?*

Unfortunately, Gerald and I were unable to discuss his prophetic pronouncement. Afterward, I returned home to Atlanta with his words reverberating in my mind.

Oddly enough, prophetic leader Paul Cain had

addressed me at that same conference. Seemingly out of nowhere he began his message by looking at me and saying, "Larry Tomczak, will you be one of my spiritual sons?"

Seated on the side of the packed auditorium, my wife and I both flinched. Sometimes you want to run, but you just can't hide. Only weeks before the conference, I had obeyed God and departed from a ministry I had founded and in which I had spent most of my Christian life. The adjustment was traumatic, to say the least. Yet I knew God had called me to move on to my next step in ministry.

In times of transition and adversity, our spiritual ears are often open to receive anything from God that will sustain and encourage us. How faithful God was to use these two men to let me know that He was still actively involved in my life—a fact I found both tremendously sustaining and encouraging.

My Refining Moment Became My Defining Moment

On the eve of my twenty-fifth anniversary in ministry, God unmistakably directed me to conclude my involvement with the ministry I had conceived, labored over and nurtured. Despite the pain and separation anxiety I felt, I also knew this was a defining moment—something we all face at least once in our lifetimes.

But why would God call me to walk away from what felt like my own flesh and blood?

To be honest, God brought me to a place where I no longer fit into the doctrine, direction and methodology of the ministry I had birthed. For years I wrestled internally with other leaders' comments stating that we were an "East Coast ministry." My heart beat for reaching the nations. Repeated attempts to bring together our apostolic base with the local church I founded were unsuccessful and left me discouraged and looking to God for answers. As time passed, my choice became painfully clear: Either remain comfortable, thus compromising my core convictions, or take a leap of faith into the next season God had for my life.

On a much deeper level, God orchestrated a series of events to bring me to my decision. He brought me through a tumultuous period of breaking during which He arrested my attention, revealed several deficiencies in my life and clarified that a season of ministry was ending.

What would people think if I concluded my season with this ministry that I was so identified with for almost my entire Christian life? I asked myself. God showed me that I was ensnared by the "fear of man" and, for too long, overly concerned about my reputation. The words of Leonard Ravenhill soon came to mind: "He who is intimate with God will never be intimidated by man."

John Kilpatrick, my friend and the spiritual overseer of the Brownsville Revival, further challenged me at the time regarding my concern for reputation: "Unless you are willing to die to your reputation, you will never enter into the full measure of God's anointing for your life."

Rather than spend the rest of my life being ruled by intimidation, behind-the-scenes "politicking" and a concern for reputation, I chose to embrace change. The time had come to walk out from under the canopy of being a people-pleaser into a new season of liberty in God. My refining moment was becoming my defining moment.

However, departing from the ministry I so dearly

loved also meant that my financial support would soon come to an end. Author Bob Mumford once said, "Living by faith is like living in the midst of a miracle *13* with one foot on the edge of disaster—if God doesn't come through for you, you go under!" How can we learn the faithfulness of God and the walk of faith unless we face periodic testing along life's way?

Fortunately for us in our time of trial, God encouraged Doris and me with an immediate supply of funds. The exact moment when I handed my secretary the letter outlining my decision to depart from my former ministry, I turned around to face my wife, her face beaming with news that came our way from a phone call literally seconds before!

"Larry, Dick Moore's attorney just called..." she began. Dick was a family friend who had died unexpectedly. Doris continued, "...and he said Dick left you $20,000 in his will! The check will be sent first thing tomorrow morning!"

My jaw dropped as I bear-hugged my wife in wide-eyed shock. "Glory to God!"

GOD CALLS US TO KEEP MOVING FORWARD

So what does all this have to do with the puzzling declaration about being "tomorrow's man?"

In *The Anointing: Three Eras*, R. T. Kendall shares the story of what inspired his outstanding, prophetic book. One day while reading 1 Samuel 16:1, a penetrating truth leaped out at him:

> The LORD said to Samuel, "How long will you mourn for Saul, since I have rejected him as king

over Israel? Fill your horn with oil and be on your way: I am sending you to Jesse of Bethlehem. I have chosen one of his sons to be king."

"In a flash," Kendall comments, "I saw three eras: yesterday's man (King Saul), today's man (Samuel), tomorrow's man (David)."[1]

For the rest of his book, Kendall challenges his readers to keep advancing with God's ongoing purposes, lest they become yesterday's people and miss out on God's purposes today. He quotes Jim Bakker, who admits:

> [I] had become yesterday's man and for years didn't know it, still moving and working in the gifts I had received in the past. God had a new message for me, a new life. God wanted to make me into tomorrow's man. That's not an easy task.[2]

Having walked through this traumatic, midlife directional change, I stand on the other side to encourage you before you come to your proverbial fork in the road. Through my own pilgrimage into the unknown I have learned that even when you are wallowing in utter stagnation and barrenness, when you are drowning in challenging circumstances and vehement criticism, the Holy Spirit can still infuse you with supernatural strength. Not strength merely to endure, but strength to enter a fresh move of God. That is, if you walk humbly, circumspectly and obediently—no matter what the cost.

THE COST OF CHANGE: BETRAYAL AND ABANDONMENT

This new change in my life was very costly. Emotional

upheaval, desertion, misunderstanding and betrayal often accompany seasons of transition. During the days prior to my departure, God gave me a distinct picture of what was to come, and He alerted me that the decision would not be well received.

Doris and I, along with one of our teenagers, were threatened in various ways if we did not cooperate with the ministry that we were leaving. We were encountering a spirit of control. We were shunned. A letter was circulated in an attempt to discredit me and to distort the events surrounding my departure. Our own family members were divided. We felt helpless, abandoned and, for the most part, alone. Our experience was very painful. It seemed like some unbelievable nightmare.

Yet the reactions we encountered shouldn't have come as a surprise. Scripture is filled with the accounts of people who suffered very painful experiences that left them broken. Jesus went through this: "I was wounded in the house of my friends" (Zech. 13:6, NKJV). The pioneer of our faith was eventually deserted by most of His closest friends. He forewarned us: "You will be betrayed even by parents, brothers, relatives and friends..." (Luke 21:16). The psalmist records, "If an enemy were insulting me, I could endure it; if a foe were raising himself against me, I could hide from him. But it is you, a man like myself, my companion, my close friend, with whom I once enjoyed sweet fellowship as we walked with the throng at the house of God" (Ps. 55:12–14).

During times of devastation when family and friends forsake us, God often cushions the blow by drawing us into His sweet presence and enveloping us in a special impartation of His grace. Because I so needed the comfort of the Holy Spirit, I opened myself to anything He had for me, and He answered the cry of my heart by giving me fresh insight and comfort from His Word, along with an unmistakable sense of the nearness of His presence.

Imagine how Joseph must have felt after he was betrayed and abandoned by his own brothers. Then he was misunderstood by his beloved master, Potiphar, and thrown into prison. There, he was forgotten by the cupbearer whom he had encouraged and befriended. (See Genesis 37–40.) Yet it was Joseph who was able to forgive, as we must also. Many years later he made the classic declaration: "You intended to harm me; but God intended it for good" (Gen. 50:20).

God May Even Be Inciting the Opposition

In the Old Testament, Shemaiah, the man of God, was told by the Lord during an insurrection against King Rehoboam, "Do not go up to fight against your brothers, the Israelites. Go home, every one of you, *for this is my doing*" (1 Kings 12:24, emphasis added).

Can God orchestrate and allow desertion and betrayal in your life? Absolutely—to take you to a new level, if you respond properly. Do you remember Job and his so-called friends? It was only when he "prayed for his friends, [that] the LORD made him prosperous again and gave him twice as much as he had before" (Job 42:10).

When Paul was abandoned during a time of opposition, how did he respond? "May it not be held against them" (2 Tim. 4:16). Some of Paul's traveling companions were with him for decades, yet they left him in his hour of need. Get ready. This test of betrayal is presented to nearly everyone.

Paul lamented his test of betrayal to Timothy, by saying, "You know that everyone in the province of Asia has deserted me, including Phygelus and Hermogenes" (2 Tim. 1:15).

"Could God be in this?" we lament. "What is going on?" Yet in Psalm 88:18 we read, "You have taken my companions and loved ones from me; the darkness is my closest friend."

THE FINISHED PRODUCT IS CONTINGENT UPON OUR RESPONSE

God often uses your experiences of betrayal and abandonment in order to refocus and refine your life and ministry—if you respond properly while you are being attacked and maligned.

> For you, O God, tested us;
>   you refined us like silver.
> You brought us into prison
>   and laid burdens on our backs.
> You let men ride over our heads;
>   we went through fire and water,
>   but you brought us to a place of abundance.
>   —PSALM 66:10–12

In the midst of God's refining process we simply cannot see the finished product—because God isn't finished with us yet. But if we persevere, someday we will be able to look back over the years and see how God refined us through testing. Eventually we will see that the betrayal and misunderstanding we experienced actually brought us to a higher level of maturity and drew us into closer communion with Him.

While the heat of this refining process was still very intense in my own life, Chip Grange, a friend of many years, challenged me not only to forgive, but to pray blessings on those who I believed had betrayed me. Paul gave similar advice to the church in Rome: "Bless those who persecute you; bless and do not curse" (Rom. 12:14).

As hard as it was, I can honestly say God gave me the grace to bless my "enemies." And to this day I can say that I continue to pray a blessing on each of my brothers by name daily.

If you have been hurt, abandoned or betrayed, you actually can cut yourself off from God's blessings when you retaliate or refuse to let the offense go. "Do not repay evil with evil or insult with insult, but with blessing, because to this you were called *so that you may inherit a blessing*" (1 Pet. 3:9, emphasis added).

Besides, if you are truly following in the ways of Jesus, opposition should come as no surprise.

> But how is it to your credit if you receive a beating for doing wrong and endure it? But if you suffer for doing good and you endure it, this is commendable before God. To this you were called, because Christ suffered for you, leaving you an example, that you should follow in his steps. "He committed no sin, and no deceit was found in his mouth." When they hurled their insults at him, he did not retaliate; when he suffered, he made no threats. Instead, he entrusted himself to him who judges justly.
> —1 PETER 2:20–23

ARE YOU TOMORROW'S MAN OR WOMAN?

You *will* face your *refining* moments—they're inevitable. But you are never guaranteed that they will become your *defining* moments. Many Christians live their entire lives as yesterday's people. They subsist on day-old manna and relish the past rather than anticipate the future. They may not even recognize the meagerness of their existence because it has become all too familiar. But deep inside they hunger for something more.

You may even be at this juncture as you read this book. But whether you are or not, I ask you: Are you tomorrow's man or woman?

Do you sense in your spirit that God is up to something in our generation? Do you ever wonder if God is attempting to use difficult, sometimes even seemingly impossible situations, to bring you—and our generation—into a new, refreshing season of the Spirit? T. D. Jakes says that if you've gone through the wringer in your spiritual development, you're a candidate to be used mightily in this present urgent hour.

The God we serve is a God of newness. His Word speaks of receiving new wine in new wineskins, enjoying a new heart, having a new name, singing a new song and proclaiming a new and living way. The words of Isaiah 43:18–19 have great significance for today: "Forget the former things; do not dwell on the past. See, I am doing a new thing! Now it springs up; do you not perceive it? I am making a way in the desert and streams in the wasteland."

But in order to enter this new season of refreshing, you must be willing to pay the price—death. Death to your agenda; death to your old habits; death to a risk-free life; death to your old selfish ways. Jesus said, "I tell you the truth, unless a kernel of wheat falls to the ground and dies, it remains only a single seed. But if it dies, it produces many seeds" (John 12:24).

Are you willing to pay the price to come into the fullness of what God ordained for your life and for His church in this historic hour?

Fortunately, the fruit of this sacrifice is nothing short of God's purpose and provision. "'For I know the plans I have for you,' declares the LORD, 'plans to prosper you and not to harm you, plans to give you hope and a future'" (Jer. 29:11).

Don't listen to Satan's manipulative lies declaring, "Your best days are behind you. God is finished with you."

Close your ears to the lies from Satan, and begin to listen to the truth from God. The best is yet to come for your life. The church's finest hour is just ahead!

Now is the time to move forward with reckless abandon and align yourself with brothers and sisters worldwide who sense that their destinies lie ahead in their calling as pioneers—not settlers.

Two

Constant Change Is Here to Stay

In 1961, at the height of the Cold War, the United States and the Soviet Union were engaged in a neck-and-neck race to achieve superiority in space. Already, dogs and monkeys had been sent into the earth's outer atmosphere. Both Soviet and American rockets had been launched—some with disastrous results. Two years earlier the USSR had aimed the Luna 1 space rocket straight at the moon—but they missed their target completely.

Now it was time for a human to fly in space for the first time in world history! Just four days before the Soviet launch date, Yuri Gagarin was chosen to fly aboard the Vostock 1. He would become the world's first space pioneer.

Moments before liftoff, while listening to music that was being piped into his command module, Yuri received word that he was being promoted to the rank of major—little comfort for a person who may not even survive the trip!

After a short delay to fix an electrical problem, the

Vostok 1 lifted off at 9:07 A.M. on April 12, 1961. While in flight, Yuri was exposed to as much as eight times the normal force of gravity on the earth. During his single orbit around the earth, Yuri conducted experiments on the effects of weightlessness on his body and on the spacecraft.

Strangely enough, Gagarin had no control over the capsule in which he was flying. Everything was automated or controlled from the ground—although he did have the code to unlock the controls so he could override the system in case of a malfunction.

Vostock 1 landed one hour and forty-eight minutes later in a field in the Soviet Union, greeted by a few cows and peasants. But when the capsule was opened, Yuri was missing! During his descent, with the capsule still four miles in the air, Yuri bailed out of Vostok 1 and descended in a separate parachute.

Yuri Gagarin returned to his people—and to the world—as a hero.

Pioneers come in all shapes and sizes. People like Jonas Salk (who developed the first polio vaccine) or Amelia Earhart (the first woman to fly solo across the Atlantic Ocean) refuse to be satisfied with the status quo.

But being a pioneer also carries with it inherent risk. During her attempt at flying around the world, Earhart and her airplane mysteriously vanished. Yuri Gagarin perished only seven years after his historic flight while conducting tests on other Soviet aircraft.

The pioneers who explored the vast North American wilderness in the 1700s and 1800s experienced similar perils. Unlike Yuri Gagarin, these early pioneers lacked the benefit of even rudimentary technology or advice from a central command center.

When the early American pioneers ventured into the unknown, they realized that the risks they were taking might exact a high cost—perhaps even their lives. But they also knew this: With the inherent risks came the potential for endless rewards.

PIONEERS VENTURE INTO THE UNKNOWN

By definition, a *pioneer* is "one who ventures into unknown or unclaimed territory to settle." Pioneers may open up new areas of thought, research or development. Pioneers are trailblazers, champions of a new order, advance agents who break new ground. They are often people who die without the respect they deserve.

The word *pioneer* comes from the French language and originally meant "a foot soldier sent on ahead to clear the way."[1] Pioneers are people who refuse to live as yesterday's people or today's people. Their feet are firmly placed in tomorrow.

As Christians, pioneers realize this world is not their home. Therefore, they live with an eternal perspective. The writer of the Book of Hebrews described men and women of faith as people with a pioneering spirit.

All these people were still living by faith when they died. They did not receive the things promised; they only saw them and welcomed them from a distance. And they admitted that they were aliens and strangers on earth. People who say such things show that they are looking for a country of their own. If they had been thinking of the country they had left, they would have had opportunity to return. Instead, they were longing for a better country—a heavenly one. Therefore God is not ashamed to be called their God, for he has prepared a city for them.

—HEBREWS 11:13–16

If you are a Christian, you follow in the footsteps of your role model, Jesus Christ:

Therefore, since we are surrounded by so great a cloud of witnesses, let us also lay aside every weight and the sin that clings so closely, and let us run with perseverance the race that is set before us, looking to *Jesus the pioneer and perfecter of our faith*, who for the sake of the joy that was set before him endured the cross, disregarding its shame, and has taken his seat at the right hand of the throne of God.

—HEBREWS 12:1–2, NRSV, EMPHASIS ADDED

When you look to Jesus, "the pioneer and perfecter of your faith," you understand that in order for revival to begin in your life, you must follow Jesus with a reckless abandon into the mysterious unknown— and that means change. Pioneering men and women of faith understand that change is the only constant.

This does not mean change for change's sake, but rather a flexibility and sensitivity to the Spirit in pioneering new ground and recovering that which has been lost due to disobedience, compromise and neglect in the church.

SETTLERS CHOOSE TO STAY BEHIND

Settlers, on the other hand, are people who settle. The word for *settle* comes from the same word as *sit*.[2] Pioneers move ahead while settlers choose to stay.

In a spiritual sense, settlers are people who settle for the status quo. They are content with yesterday's manna and whatever leftovers life gives them.

Someone has said that the seven last words of a dying church are: "We've never done it that way before." Such a church is willing to settle. Any church—whether contemporary or traditional in worship style—can easily settle into a rut. And churches aren't the only entities that wrestle with this problem—people do, too.

If you truly hunger for personal and corporate revival, as I do, God may require of you what He required of me. I had to take a hard look at myself to identify my comfort zones. Then, God required me to renounce any tendencies I had to stay in those comfort zones. You must do this also. Then, and only then, will you be prepared to forge ahead with God's ongoing purpose in your generation.

Capture the pioneering spirit of our forefather David, of whom it is recorded, "For when David had served God's purpose in his own generation, he fell asleep" (Acts 13:36).

CULTIVATING THE PIONEERING SPIRIT

"Larry, Marnie died this morning as she was getting ready for church! She had an aneurysm. Would...would you...help us with some type of memorial service?"

The phone call that shattered my Sunday evening

calm came (as I was writing this book) from a dear friend whose only daughter unexpectedly "went home" to be with the Lord. She was thirty-one years old. Married for seven years with no children, Marnie had struggled with drugs for fifteen years until she was instantaneously set free fifteen months prior.

What happened? I'm not referring to her "homecoming," which remains a mystery, but the miraculous deliverance she experienced. What brought about that deliverance?

Marnie had a direct revelation from Jesus Christ while driving to work one morning that arrested her attention and turned her completely around. Her car shook. She pulled off the road. She was shaken to the core for three days. From that point on, she was never the same.

Upon phoning her father at work a few hours after the Lord "visited" her, Marnie conveyed an urgent message that her dad, an international consultant, jotted down and subsequently read at his daughter's memorial service.

Bob stood center stage as grief blanketed him and tears welled up in his eyes. "Marnie told me that Jesus said the time is very short. Judgment is at hand. We must reach as many as possible with the gospel of salvation."

Bob looked seriously into the collective eyes of all assembled and repeated, "The time is short. This was the message God wanted Marnie to convey to us all."

While no man "knows neither the day nor the hour" of Christ's return, we are instructed to be watchful and not be ignorant "of the times and seasons" (Matt. 25:13; 1 Thess. 5:1). We are told, "But you, brothers, are not in darkness so that this day should surprise you like a thief"

(1 Thess. 5:4). Jesus chastened those in His day, "You know how to interpret the appearance of the sky, but you cannot interpret the signs of the times" (Matt. 16:3).

Today we must be like the "men of Issachar, who understood the times and knew what Israel should do" (1 Chron. 12:32).

Prophetic leader Paul Cain said recently, "The time of His return is not immediate, but it is imminent!"

YOU MUST CONTINUE MOVING FORWARD WITH GOD

Years ago I deplaned at Los Angeles International Airport and proceeded to the baggage claim. Walking briskly next to a moving sidewalk I engaged in a game with an unsuspecting businessman. While he was being carried along by the sidewalk in motion, I walked beside him, trying to keep pace.

At one point, I noticed that my shoelace was untied. I stopped, bent over, tied the shoe and proceeded to reenter my little game, picking up right where I had left off—or so I thought. As I stood up, I realized that the man had continued moving ahead while I had been stationary for the moment. By the time I was ready to continue, my unsuspecting friend was long gone!

Your walk with God is similar to my airport experience. God is neither static nor stagnant—He's always on the move. Genesis 1:2 says that "the Spirit of God was hovering over the waters," and He has never stopped hovering. The Bible states that "the eyes of the LORD run to and fro throughout the whole earth, to show Himself strong on behalf of those whose heart is loyal to Him" (2 Chron. 16:9, NKJV).

What lesson can be learned from all of this? If you want to become a man and woman of faith, you must keep moving! The moment you stop, you get left behind. You cannot hesitate even for a moment in your relationship with the God you love and serve.

The vast majority of people who colonized the East Coast of North America during the 1600s and 1700s were pioneers. However, over time many of these people became satisfied with the settled life. They bartered their lives of adventure and challenge for safety and stability. Just because you were a pioneer in the past is no guarantee that you will be a pioneer in the future.

Jonathan Edwards, a pioneer church leader during the Great Awakening of the 1700s, put it this way: "The task of every generation is to discover in what direction the Sovereign Redeemer is moving, then to move in that direction."

To be a pioneer and not a settler necessitates being flexible and willing to change. It means honoring the new millennium beatitude: "Blessed are the flexible— they shall not be broken."

Are you hungry for God's presence? Are you desperate for more of Him, or are you content to stay where you are?

THE NEW WINE REALLY IS BETTER!

Jesus clearly understood that many people in His culture were satisfied with status quo.

> He told them this parable: "No one tears a patch from a new garment and sews it on an old one. If he does, he will have torn the new garment, and the patch from the new will not match the old.

28

And no one pours new wine into old wineskins. If he does, the new wine will burst the skins, the wine will run out and the wineskins will be ruined. No, new wine must be poured into new wineskins. And no one after drinking old wine wants the new, for he says, 'The old is better.'"

—LUKE 5:36–39

A common misconception in our society is that old wine is better than new wine. This may be true, but only under ideal conditions: The wine must be of very high quality, it must be well sealed, and it must be preserved away from the sun at fifty degrees Fahrenheit. Was this possible in Jesus' day? Hardly. Even under optimal conditions today, many wines begin to turn sour after only seven years.

In this passage, Jesus was saying that many people become satisfied with wine that has turned sour. Rather than taste new wine, many people content themselves with "the same old same old."

Let's face reality. The church for which our Lord Jesus gave His life, and in which He is committed to establish purity and power so the gates of hell will not prevail against it, is again in need of the taste of new wine. (See Matthew 16:18.) So easily we become satisfied with the old, soured wine of previous moves of God. So quickly we lose our taste for something new.

God has been pouring out His new wine of the Spirit for centuries. But like the manna the children of Israel consumed in the wilderness, over time it grows old. Stale. Sour.

What we need is *revival*, **which means "to make alive again." Revival is the extraordinary move of the Holy Spirit, which**

produces extraordinary results. Revival turns sour wine into new wine and old worm-infested manna into the bread of life.

30 If you honestly assess yourself and your church as anemic, irrelevant, compromised or lacking in God's manifest presence and power, you are a candidate to see God intervene in your life. Historically, God proves Himself as committed to revival!

Paul Cain said that the Toronto Blessing, with its emphasis on the Father's love, was the "gentle awakening." Pensacola, with its repentance base, was the "rude awakening." But there's yet to come another "Great Awakening" prior to the return of our Lord!

I, for one, want to be a part of the next move of God. I believe you do, too, or you wouldn't be reading this book.

YOUR PAST PROPELS YOU INTO THE FUTURE

In order to leave the barren wilderness and venture into God's land of promise, you will need to follow the Israelites' example and move when the cloud moves. This requires that you truly live by faith like the great men and women of old. Our natural tendency is to make choices that ensure safety, familiarity and comfort. But faith flourishes when you leave behind your comfortable surroundings.

Does this mean that you should forget the past entirely? No. The words of George Santayana serve as a reminder to us all: "Those who cannot remember the past are condemned to repeat it."

God is enlisting an army of men and women who fit

the description of the teacher of the law about which Jesus spoke in Matthew 13:52: "Therefore every teacher of the law who has been instructed about the kingdom of heaven is like the owner of a house who brings out of his storeroom new treasures as well as old." Notice the order. It's not taking the old and seeing if the new fits. We take the new and have to see if the old still fits. That's a big difference.

31

There is value in the old—but there are new treasures God wants to make known to the pioneers of today. Don't invalidate the new by clinging to the old. Jesus rebuked the Pharisees who chose to "nullify the word of God for the sake of your tradition"(Matt. 15:6).

God has strategically placed you at a juncture in history between the achievements of the past and the awesome potential of the uncharted future. Now is the time to learn from yesterday, listen to what God is saying today and look forward to what He wants you to accomplish tomorrow.

Beware of being taken captive by your past or becoming so enraptured with the present that you settle and miss out. You have the spiritual DNA of a visionary people! God is calling out men and women to be trailblazers . . . forerunners . . . servants who go first in order to pave the way for a new outpouring of God's Spirit. He wants you to inspire others to join you on the adventure of a lifetime.

On Yuri Gagarin's maiden voyage, the first-phase booster rocket that propelled his capsule through space reached a point where it was no longer functional. Not only did it provide dead weight to the rocket, but the excess material posed a fire hazard on his descent.

In a similar way, God used the Jesus People and Charismatic movements of the '60s and '70s and the Toronto and Pensacola visitations in recent times as boosters propelling millions into a new dimension of the Spirit. Without them, we would not be where we are today. However, if you live in the past moves of God, if you yearn for that old-time religion, they will serve as dead weight and actually pose as barriers to what God wants to accomplish next in your life.

CAN I MISS GOD?

This begs the question: Can people actually miss out on the next move of God?

Consider the Israelites who spent forty years in the wilderness while on a journey that should have taken only eleven days![3] Instead of pressing onward in step with the cloud, the Israelites grumbled and longed for the security and familiarity of their former life. As a result, only Caleb and Joshua, men who had a "different spirit," entered into their inheritance (Num. 14:24).

Second Kings 18 records the account of King Hezekiah, whom God used to spark revival in his day. We read in verses 3 and 4, "[Hezekiah] did what was right in the eyes of the LORD, just as his father David had done...He broke into pieces the bronze snake Moses had made..."

Why would this please God? Earlier hadn't God moved dynamically through the bronze serpent to bring healing to the ailing children of Israel? (See Numbers 21.) Yes, but now, seven hundred years later, the people were worshiping it. The passage continues,

" . . . for up to that time the Israelites had been burning incense to it" (v. 4).

When you cling sentimentally to previous moves of God, you can, in effect, worship the move of God rather than God Himself. In the end, your actions hinder the work of the Holy Spirit in your life. Once King Hezekiah removed the barrier, however, God's Spirit was poured out.

33

The Ability to Change Isn't Limited to the Young

While it's true you can't stay young forever, you can remain youthful in spirit. Read the words an eighty-five-year-old Caleb spoke to Joshua:

> Now then, just as the LORD promised, he has kept me alive for forty-five years since the time he said this to Moses, while Israel moved about in the desert. So here I am today, eighty-five years old! I am still as strong today as the day Moses sent me out; I'm just as vigorous to go out to battle now as I was then. Now give me this hill country that the LORD promised me that day. You yourself heard then that the Anakites were there and their cities were large and fortified, but, the LORD helping me, I will drive them out just as he said.
> —JOSHUA 14:10–12

Caleb demonstrated the heart of a spiritual pioneer. Spiritual pioneers—some who are even older in age as was Caleb—still exist today. At the time I wrote this book, my wife's parents, ages eighty and seventy-seven, are energetic leaders in our local church. They continue to model for me the spirit of a pioneer even in old age!

Don't risk waking up some morning at the end of your life to lament, *I blew it! I didn't keep in step with the Spirit, and I missed the purpose of God in my generation!* Press on with the pioneering spirit, or you may risk missing a fresh move of God in your life.

34

GOD IS MERGING TWO GENERATIONS TO IMPACT THE NEXT

Today a new breed of men and women is emerging! God is bringing together two generations that will transform this present decadent society. You can be counted among the men and women who are becoming an Elijah generation in a King Ahab and Jezebel age.

Prior to the first coming of our Lord, God sent John the Baptist in an Elijah-type ministry:

> Many of the people of Israel will he bring back to the Lord their God. And he will go on before the Lord, in the spirit and power of Elijah, to turn the hearts of the fathers to their children and the disobedient to the wisdom of the righteous—to make ready a people prepared for the Lord.
> —LUKE 1:16–17

This was the beginning of the fulfillment of Malachi 4:5–6, which is also the last promise of the Old Testament:

> See, I will send you the prophet Elijah before that great and dreadful day of the LORD comes. He will turn the hearts of the fathers to their children, and the hearts of the children to their fathers; or else I will come and strike the land with a curse.

If you look closely, you will notice that the end of the age will be preceded by the restoration of the fathers and the children. Since the end of the age (the "great and dreadful day of the LORD") hasn't occurred, the completion of this promise is yet to come.

Today we are witnessing what I believe is not a fad but a legitimate move of God—intergenerational ministry. Dads and moms from the baby-boomer generation (those people born between 1946 and 1964) are joining with their sons and daughters in an all-out spiritual war!

Many of us who are fathers and sons experienced a taste of this firsthand during the Promise Keepers' Million Man Solemn Assembly a few years ago. Others experienced The Call D.C., where over three hundred thousand parents and youth gathered on the Mall in Washington, D.C. in September 2000 for a day of fasting, worship and prayer as described in Joel 2:15–16:

> Blow the trumpet in Zion,
>   declare a holy fast,
>   call a sacred assembly.
> Gather the people,
>   consecrate the assembly;
> bring together the elders,
>   gather the children,
>   those nursing at the breast.

God is going to have His way! A new generation of Spirit-filled men and women is emerging on the horizon. They're filled with the fire of God and are hungry for more of His life-changing presence. Onward they march, unwilling to settle for yesterday's blessings. They are pioneers who are hoisting their sails and moving where the Spirit is blowing.

In 1983, a fledgling computer company with an odd name, Apple, was experiencing growing pains. Steve Jobs, the twenty-eight-year-old cofounder, realized the need to hire the most qualified individual he could find to run his company. His search landed him in the office of John Sculley, the CEO of the Pepsi Corporation.

At that time Pepsi was a behemoth compared to tiny Apple Computers, and, at first, Sculley seemed uninterested in risking his important position with an international company for a little-known, risky operation. Then Jobs asked him a haunting question. "Do you want to spend the rest of your life selling sugared water, or do you want a chance to change the world?"

Sculley chose to change the world.[4]

Before you lies a choice. Do you want to spend the rest of your life pursuing the safe existence of a settler, or do you want to change the world? Being a history-maker begins with an openness to change. The pioneer understands that the adage "Constant change is here to stay" is not a cliché but a way of life in the kingdom of God.

God has a thrilling life in store for you. Now is your time to rendezvous with destiny! Embrace the call, and, with humility and passion, display the reckless abandon needed to catapult you into your next step in God.

Three

Where God Guides, He Provides

Doris, everything I've given myself to in my twenty-five years of ministry is basically over."

"Larry... Larry... God hasn't abandoned us! He's a faithful God. He's up to something. Look, financially we'll be OK. We can cut lawns or, even though it sounds funny, if all six of us donate blood each month, we can bring in enough money. I figured it out—we can get by... "

Standing face to face in the early morning solitude of our basement, my wife and I exchanged random thoughts and stared into one another's teary eyes knowing a chapter had closed. The moment was both frightening and bittersweet, yet inwardly we knew that if a chapter was coming to a close, a new chapter was about to begin.

THE FAITHFULNESS OF GOD

The decision to move on to the next step in our pilgrimage brought a Scripture passage to mind: "By faith

Abraham...obeyed and went, even though he did not know where he was going" (Heb. 11:8). Like Abraham, we left the safe surroundings of family and friends to venture into the unknown. We didn't know where we were going—we didn't even know where our next dollar was going to come from.

The life of a pioneer can at times appear romantic— the excitement of discovery, the thrill of adventure, the challenge of battling the odds and the rewards that follow the risk. But every pioneer must also face the harsh reality that blazing a new trail may mean leaving family, friends and a secure life, just as Abraham did.

A TIME OF CONFIRMATION

The day after our momentous decision to depart our former ministry, I found myself numb yet relieved as I shared lunch with David VanCronkite, a dear friend who leads an inner-city ministry in Atlanta called "Blood-N-Fire."

"Tomorrow night we are hosting a leaders' gathering with a gifted prophetess named Jill Austin. Why don't you and Doris come?" David asked in his winsome way.

"Why not!"

The next evening Doris and I slipped in the back of a medium-size room simply to listen to this bright and bubbly lady minister to David's folks. After sharing the Word, she was about to conclude the gathering when she flinched, seemingly reconnected on a spiritual track, and transitioned to a time of personal prophetic ministry.

"Will she call me out of the fifty or so assembled?" I mused. I engaged my microcassette recorder just in case this woman whom I had never seen or heard before called me forth.

Suddenly, she glanced our way and said, "The fellow with the pink shirt and black vest...come up here with your wife."

I switched on the recorder as Jill's eyes twinkled and her smile gave way to a confident grin. Then she spoke.

"Transition...I sense transition. It's a time of change. You're coming out of some ministry with just the clothes on your back. It's a God-thing. It's about integrity. You are people who want to follow the fresh wind of My Spirit. You have said, 'If whatever we are part of becomes too traditional, then we want to leave in order to follow the fresh wind of the Spirit.' Don't let people camp around you. I am going to place you in the hot spots of the nations. Know it is I who am doing this."

Not long thereafter, I received separate invitations to visit three "hot spots" of revival activity that were destined to impact my life profoundly.

First, a call came one day from Dr. Michael Brown, president of the newly founded Brownsville Revival School of the Ministry in Pensacola, Florida. He said he sensed he should invite me to visit the revival along with my wife and family. I shared with him the recent events and inquired if he'd ever gone through a similar time of upheaval and breaking.

He related how earlier in his ministry he came to a place where he wrongly longed for theological respectability and immersed himself in the same doctrinal direction from which I had withdrawn. "God lovingly chastened me," he related, "for intellectual pride. I came face to face with the reality that subtly I had lost my first love for Jesus along with my passion for prayer and reaching the lost." Oh, how I identified with his experience.

Our trip to the Brownsville Revival revolutionized our lives. It set the stage for the privilege of becoming a part of the faculty where weekly I began teaching in the midst of eleven hundred radical students (two of whom soon included my children).

Second, during lunch one day, an apostolic leader named John Kelly invited me to accompany him to the "hot bed" of spiritual activity in Argentina, where a fifteen-year revival was in progress. It was from here that Steve Hill, the evangelist in Brownsville, had been launched.

The third "hot spot" was my visit to Pasadena, California, for a Harvest Rock/H.I.M. Ministries conference, already mentioned in the previous chapter. My closest ministry friend for twenty-five years, Che Ahn, who serves in leadership for this network of churches, phoned me upon my departure from the former ministry and invited Doris and me to be their guests in this emerging center of spiritual activity. Two years prior, Che and prophetic leader Lou Engle had left the same movement of which I had been a part and were catapulted into a new dimension of ministry and fruitfulness. (Lou Engle colabors with Che and was used by God to convey a vision of the Holy Spirit for The Call D.C., a multigenerational gathering of over three hundred thousand youth and parents in September of 2000. This gathering interceded and worshiped God on the Mall of our nation's capital during several days.)

From my experience, I have learned that as God stirs His people to move into their next assignment, He will supernaturally provide as He guides. Advancement will

often be met with opposition and "stretch" us to our limits, but if we can stand the pull, He'll pull us through!

GOD LEADS FROM *BEHIND*

During this transitional time, God repeatedly sustained me with these words:

41

> Although the Lord gives you the bread of adversity and the water of affliction, your teachers will be hidden no more; with your own eyes you will see them. Whether you turn to the right or to the left, your ears will hear a voice behind you, saying, "This is the way; walk in it."
>
> —ISAIAH 30:20–21

Notice that the voice comes from *behind*. The tendency is to wait passively for God to *lead* the way and to give a supernatural sign before moving ahead. This requires no faith. On the contrary, God speaks and calls you to take a step of faith, often before you see any sign of His supernatural intervention.

The very week I ended my ministry ties, I ran into John Beckett, president of Intercessors for America (I serve on their board), at the PromiseKeepers' Million Man gathering on the Mall in Washington, D.C.

After exchanging pleasantries and quickly catching up on each other's lives, John offered to pray for me. There surrounded by a million men, I was stunned by God's providence as John lifted up these words: "Father, we thank You that You promised in Your Word that whether we turn to the right or to the left, we would hear a voice behind us saying, 'This is the way; walk in it.'"

The Life of a Pioneer Is a Walk of Faith

Despite the uncertainty of our future, I decided to respond in faith because "without faith it is impossible to please God" (Heb. 11:6). Fear paralyzes; faith propels. Sometimes you need to keep moving forward even when you don't know where you're headed. "You need to persevere so that when you have done the will of God, you will receive what he has promised" (Heb. 10:36). As I sought to follow the voice behind me as I walked through our stormy transition, I discovered God's wonderful, supernatural provision.

God may be nudging you to move into a new frontier in your life or ministry, and you may be hesitant to respond due to very real considerations:

"I've invested five...ten...fifteen years into this position."

"I have three children, and they're getting older."

"How will I pay the bills?"

"What would people think?"

"What if I'm blackballed for leaving?"

While it's important to resist acting hastily or moving ahead of your spouse or responding in some totally irresponsible manner, a faith-exercising, risk-taking step is essential to discovering the new frontier God has for you.

By the time we started our lives over again, I had invested twenty-five years into one ministry. Due to the time and energy I had dedicated to this ministry and the nature of my departure, the vast majority of my connections suddenly dried up. We had no stable source of income, no severance package, no social security (like many ministers, I opted out twenty years before) and no medical insurance to go along with a hefty house payment and ongoing bills.

But the moment we made our blind yet bold step of faith, we began to see God intervene in our lives like never before.

43

Often it isn't until you take that first step of faith before you discover God's faithfulness. When He speaks—and you obey—He will supply what you need to carry out that step of obedience. If you ever feel a little timid about taking that first step of faith in a real-life pioneering situation, then you'll be encouraged by some of the miracles I'm about to share, miracles that God worked on Doris' and my behalf. These miracles witness to the faithfulness of the God who guides and provides for His pioneers:

> ∽ As I mentioned earlier, the moment I finished writing my letter explaining my decision to conclude the season of involvement in the former ministry, we were informed that we had inherited $20,000 from a deceased friend.

> ∽ A longtime friend and fellow worker in the Lord offered to pay our health insurance premiums for our family as long as we needed.

> ∽ A friend asked Doris and me to visit him in his home. We thought he wanted us to minister to him in his battle with cancer. Instead, he presented us with a sizable check to undergird us in our new phase. Shortly thereafter he went home to be with the Lord.

> ∽ Different Christian leaders and longtime friends, both here in America and abroad, called to encourage us and tell us that sizable checks were on the way. Some offered to support us

as long as we needed it! One brother said the Lord laid me on his heart while in prayer and prompted him to send us a generous check, income he earned while working on a promo for the surprisingly successful Tae Bo exercise video.

WOULD MY LIFE IN MINISTRY BE DESTROYED BY A MAGAZINE ARTICLE?

Immediately following my departure from the former ministry, I felt completely disoriented, and I struggled against Satan's incessant lies: "You're finished." "Your best days are behind you." "Your reputation is shot." I knew I was in a battle. God used two significant events to encourage me and thrust me through Satan's first line of attack.

First, Mike Bickle, a longtime friend and respected Christian leader who was launching his International House of Prayer initiative, not only called repeatedly to encourage me, but he invited me to explore prayerfully with him the possibility of my becoming the new senior pastor of his church in Kansas City. Although God later made it clear that this wasn't the direction we were to pursue, being considered to lead this tremendous church felt like a vote of confidence!

Second, I began hearing reports that *Charisma* magazine was preparing a story on my ministry change. Someone working in their office gave me a "heads up" on comments passed on to them that were meant to discredit me and misrepresent my situation. My thoughts began racing, *Would their well-intentioned editor feature a story that distorts what is already a devastating event in my life?*

Amidst the buzz and developments unfolding around

me, I have to admit that I fought daily battles with fear over this one. Would I be portrayed as an angry leader obsessed with a spirit of independence and rebellion? Would all my years of ministry and my quest to walk in integrity be destroyed because of a single magazine article?

Then one Saturday afternoon, I walked to the mailbox to get my mail, and my eyes settled on an envelope with the *Charisma* logo in the upper left-hand corner.

A cold chill ran down my spine, *Is this the advance copy of a negative article in the next issue? Lord, what's happening now?*

I took a deep breath and lifted a silent prayer as I paused on my driveway to slowly open the letter. Here is what I read:

> The day I heard about the action taken against you the Lord gave me a vision as I prayed. You were lying on the ground, and all around there were tiny little men running around trying to pin you down with little threads. It was just like a scene out of *Gulliver's Travels*. You were lying helpless on the ground while these miniature men were holding you hostage.
>
> When I saw this in the spirit, I instantly understood that these men were powerless to hold you down. Their efforts were puny and of no consequence. I knew that God was calling you to rise up and throw off these tiny restraints. They are just threads, and they have no power over you.
>
> Please know that I am praying for you as you rise up and find your rightful place in leadership. God has an awesome call on your life, Larry. I am 100

percent behind you. Although we don't know each other that well, you spoke into my life regularly during my early days. You are a hero in my book. I know God has great things in store for you and your family.

46

Please call me if there is ever anything I can do for you.

SINCERELY,
J. LEE GRADY, EDITOR
CHARISMA MAGAZINE

There on the driveway in front of my house, a tremendous burden was lifted off my shoulders!

LUXURY ITEMS HAVE NO PLACE IN THE LIFE OF A PIONEER

When God moves you on to your next assignment, you can be assured that it will be accompanied by tests and challenges. But God also promises to supply you with the means to overcome them. (See Philippians 4:19.) Not only did God do this for me on a personal level, but He also provided the resources to plant a church— one of God's next steps for me.

Starting a church again from scratch in my basement was a humbling experience after my years in ministry, but it was absolutely essential in order for God to transition me to a higher level. He had to break me and dismantle all my idols—as well as the areas of security that had gradually crept into my life. To go further and deeper, He had to once again bring me back to the place where I knew anything good in my life came solely from Him.

When pioneers embark on a new adventure, they know that luxury items have no place in their possessions. Only essential items can accompany them. In the same way, God required that I rid myself of any rings or jewelry (i.e., accomplishments, abilities, favor or spiritual fruit) that would tempt me to think that I was responsible for my success.

47

Jesus is a jealous bridegroom. When you begin to drift from the absolute centrality and preeminence of Jesus...When you find yourself giving more to the work of the Lord than the Lord of the work...When you sense God withdrawing the consciousness of His presence and allowing you to experience what early Christian mystics referred to as "the dark night of the soul"...there is a good chance our loving Lord is preparing you for a shift that is about to take place that will be painful but necessary to pioneer new ground. Yet in the process, He will return you to your true husband and lover—Jesus!

Have you drifted? Do you sense God is blocking your path? Have you been admiring the rings or jewelry in your possession? Perhaps you are being delivered back to intimacy with your true Husband and Lover.

The Old Testament Book of Hosea is the story of a jilted, lovesick God who uses any means necessary to win back the heart of His wandering lover (Israel) to Himself.

> "She decked herself with rings and jewelry, and went after her lovers, but me she forgot," declares the LORD. "Therefore I am now going to allure her; I will lead her into the desert and speak tenderly to

48

her. There I will give her back her vineyards, and will make the Valley of Achor a door of hope. There she will sing as in the days of her youth, as in the day she came up out of Egypt. In that day," declares the LORD, "you will call me 'my husband'; you will no longer call me 'my master.'"

—HOSEA 2:13–16

As God allured me back to Himself, I discovered a new appreciation for the depths of His grace and the wonder of His supply.

GOD GAVE US A TRIPLE NEW BEGINNING!

By the time we had grown to twenty families, God made clear it was time to move our fledgling church out of the basement and into a home of its own. Miraculously, God supplied our need of $25,000 to move into a former karate studio with a $50,000 offering—on one Sunday, with only one week to pray and prepare!

Moving into our new church home was exciting, but the needed renovations required a great deal of money and labor. After only a few months our financial resources were depleted. Standing before the assembled gathering of the new Christ the King church one Sunday morning, I confessed the reality of our situation: "Folks, we are simply out of money!"

After preaching the Word and praying together, we received an offering that blew everyone away— $16,000. An unbelieving gentleman who was visiting dropped a check in the offering for $10,000!

That night we hosted a special area-wide gathering featuring John Kilpatrick, who pastored the Brownsville Revival in Pensacola, Florida. Because of his late arrival to the evening service, we had no time to talk before I introduced him. Near the end of his message on "The Suddenlies of God," Pastor Kilpatrick stopped suddenly and announced, "I believe God wants me to do something that I hardly ever do—receive an offering for this new church."

Forgoing his honorarium and inviting people to deposit their offering in a baby's car seat that he placed in the front, I stood in utter amazement. The tally: $16,000! And the next morning at a leaders' get-together with about a hundred people present, John did it again—without any encouragement from me. The tally: $16,000, again!

Within twenty-four hours we went from zero to $48,000—and all I could do was give glory to God. Pastor Kilpatrick told me, "Larry, the number eight in Scripture signifies a new beginning, and God gave you eight multiplied by two, three separate times. I'd say He's calling you to a triple new beginning!"

Up to that point, our church plant had endured fourteen months without any live worship, except for a few guests. Week after week I coordinated the songs; that meant I organized and played worship CDs through our sound system. Humbling—yes. A test of faith and perseverance—absolutely.

My reason for not having a worship leader wasn't because no one offered to lead or because no one in our congregation had any skills. But I sensed God was doing some fresh things in His church and wanted to do things *His* way, in *His* time, with *His* criteria for nonperformance worship ministry in this new move of God.

The same night that Pastor Kilpatrick spoke on "The Suddenlies of God," God brought into our midst Matt Tommey, an anointed, gifted worship leader who had just walked through a tremendous breaking experience of his own. As Matt was learning to lead worship in a biblical, nonperforming way at his previous church, his pastor determined that his style of worship was "too intimate," and he was abruptly let go.

Not only did God perform a financial miracle that night, but He answered our prayer with a "suddenly" of God. Now we have an anointed worship leader who came to us in *His* way, in *His* time, with *His* criteria.

GOD IS A RESPECTER OF *FAITH*

Where God guides, He provides. When God speaks, He supplies. As God calls you to step out of the boat like Peter, and you obey with your eyes focused on Jesus, you'll be amazed at the ways He supplies your needs.

Peter had to take a step of faith in order to walk on the water. In the same way, God requires bold steps of faith before you will discover if the water will support you or not. Derek Prince says, "Every step of progress in the Christian life must come by faith."

While God is no respecter of persons, He is a respecter of faith. The late Apostle of Faith, Smith Wigglesworth, once said, "There's something about believing God that will cause Him to pass over a million people to get to you!"

You see, you don't *determine* your destiny; you *discover*

it. And you discover your destiny as you walk by faith, continually seeking God and moving forward, no matter how challenging the path. Remember the classic line in the baseball movie *The Rookie*: "It's OK to think about what you want to be until you realize what you were meant to be." The appointing brings the anointing!

51

> Then the LORD replied: "Write down the revelation and make it plain on tablets *so that a herald may run with it.* For the revelation awaits an appointed time; it speaks of the end and will not prove false. Though it linger, wait for it; it will certainly come and will not delay. See, he is puffed up; his desires are not upright—*but the righteous will live by his faith.*
> —HABAKKUK 2:2–4, EMPHASIS ADDED

By walking humbly in obedience, God will provide you with the strength and encouragement to finish what He called you to do—even when it appears that all the "doors" around you have apparently closed. "He who began a good work in you will carry it on to completion until the day of Christ Jesus" (Phil. 1:6).

IF YOU CAN STAND THE PULL, GOD WILL PULL YOU THROUGH

From my experience, I learned that God supernaturally provides *as* He guides—not a minute sooner. As you walk forward and listen to the voice behind you, God will tell you what way to go.

I also learned that advancements are often met with opposition. You may feel stretched to the limit, but if you can stand the pull, God will pull you through!

We read in Isaiah 61:3 that God bestows upon those who grieve in Zion (in other words, those hurting people who belong to Him) a "crown of beauty instead of ashes, the oil of gladness instead of mourning, and a garment of praise instead of a spirit of despair."

52

Your past, present or future experiences may not be as dramatic as mine, but I assure you that when God guides you forward, it will not be without trauma or pain. Jesus promised that in this world you *will* have tribulation (John 16:33). However, in the process He also transforms your ashes into a crown of beauty—if you allow Him to do so. But in order for this to happen, you must be willing to obey God's will for your life, no matter what the price—reputation, position, financial security, comfort or convenience.

Have you gone through a painful season where family, friends or fellow-laborers in the kingdom left you feeling ripped off, isolated and misunderstood? Have you obeyed God's will for your life by forgiving them?

Through the difficult experiences you may have suffered, God may be stirring you to move onto a higher plane and into a fresh season in the Spirit. If so, be assured that the same God who stirs you will also catch you and carry you in this lifestyle of reckless abandon.

> ...like an eagle that stirs up its nest and hovers over its young, that spreads its wings to catch them and carries them on its pinions. The LORD alone led him...He made him ride on the heights of the land
> —DEUTERONOMY 32:11–13

Next to this passage in my Bible appear the words: "God's manual for maturity." You may feel that God is calling you to jump out of the safe confines of your cozy nest. You may even look over the edge and be unable to see where you will land. But once you are in a free fall, God will catch you, and if you allow Him, He will use the process to build your faith.

If you sense God stirring you to jump out of the nest, what are you waiting for? Ask for wisdom (James 1:5). Seek anointed counsel, and trust Him to show you how to proceed with your next step. "The steps of a good man are ordered by the LORD" (Ps. 37:23, NKJV).

Do you want to grow old dreaming about what life could have been, or would you rather enjoy the adventure right now—with no regrets?

Success in life is not about accumulating things. It's about fulfilling your destiny and becoming all God intended you to be. Don't miss it because of a past disappointment, hurt or sinful reaction.

YOUR PAST IS PREPARATION FOR YOUR FUTURE

While God was intervening in my life in such a dramatic way, I sensed He was going to use my experiences to motivate others to launch out into the deep for their next assignment from God.

During this season, God used Derek Brown, an apostolic leader from Great Britain, to encourage me to pioneer into the glorious unknown. During a message he preached one evening, I listened as he recounted the breaking period he had gone through and how the Lord assured him of His care: "My son, the previous thirty years of your Christian life have simply been preparation for what is to come!"

My many years as a father, husband and Christian leader were culminating in this next step. When you can see your life as preparation for the next thing God has for you, then you will be much more willing to weather the inevitable storms that take place during your periodic seasons of transition.

Seasons of transition usually bring turbulence and instability, so it's important that you move forward carefully and purposefully. Satan drives; the Shepherd guides. And even though new levels bring new devils, God is committed to providing for you at every turn, because "he who began a good work in you will carry it on to completion until the day of Christ Jesus" (Phil. 1:6).

Are you ready to move forward into God's unique plan for your life? Then keep moving ahead while listening to the voice that speaks to you from behind. You may not know where you're going, but be encouraged that God will lead you into new adventures and provide for you in ways beyond imagination. It all begins with the first step—followed by another...and then another.

Four

Restoration: It Will Happen!

The Almighty certainly never intended that people should travel at such a breakneck speed."

New York Governor Martin Van Buren penned these words in the winter of 1829 to warn against a grave national danger: the railroad. His letter to President Jackson pointed out the obvious hazards.

> As you may well know, Mr. President, "railroad" carriages are pulled at the enormous speed of 15 miles per hour by "engines" which, in addition to endangering life and limb of passengers, roar and snort their way through the countryside, setting fire to crops, scaring the livestock and frightening the women and children.

Van Buren preferred the canal boat. It was safer, more dependable and already tested. It worked. No risks. In his opinion, the canal system was absolutely essential for the nation's welfare.

Had President Jackson listened to Van Buren's advice,

modern transportation would be quite different than it is today. Manhattan executives would line up on the docks after work to take the canal boat across town. Taxi drivers would paddle passengers in canoes through rush-hour spray. The Dodge Viper would be nothing more than a dream...or a nightmare.

56

And the 747 jumbo jet? "If God wanted man to fly He'd have given him wings!" That was the sarcastic response of the father of the Wright brothers when asked about his sons' efforts to invent the airplane. Ironically, this man was also a Methodist bishop.

A precursory look at world history demonstrates that progress is inevitable. You may object to the advent of the railroad, the airplane or the computer, but regardless of your opinion, no matter how hard you may try to stand in their way, you just can't stop them. And as time passes, the rate of progress seems to accelerate at exponential proportions.

THE WORLD IS A STAGE; HISTORY IS THE DRAMA; AND WE ARE THE PERFORMERS

In a similar way, God is unfolding His purposes. You may stand in His way, but you cannot prevent the inevitable fulfillment of His Word. As time passes, world events seem to increase in intensity as do our visitations from God. God isn't changing, but His purposes are unfolding quickly.

In this chapter you will discover that the purposes of God have been unfolding since the beginning of time. Like a divine drama that culminates with a spectacular climax, God is restoring His church. If you belong to

Jesus you need not be afraid because you can know with assurance how this drama will end. And never forget that you know the playwright—almighty God.

In the greatest story ever told we witness what is, at times, a love story, an action adventure, a tragedy, a comedy, but above all, a mystery. And the performers in this production are the men and women on the front lines in the battle between good and evil. They are the pioneers of light and darkness. They aren't content with what already exists; they look ahead to new directions, new solutions. Those men and women who pledge their allegiance to Jesus Christ know that the degree of their success will depend upon the extent that they know their Commander-in-Chief.

YOUR CALLING IS TO KNOW GOD AND FULFILL HIS PLANS FOR YOUR LIFE

Even before you were born, God composed the role you are to play in His divine drama. The psalmist wrote, "All the days ordained for me were written in your book before one of them came to be" (Ps. 139:16).

The apostle Paul clearly understood that the key to fulfilling God's purposes for your life lay in knowing Jesus: "I want to know Christ and the power of his resurrection and the fellowship of sharing in his sufferings, becoming like him in his death, and so, somehow, to attain to the resurrection from the dead" (Phil. 3:10–11). As a Christian, your highest calling is to know God and, out of intimate, personal union with Him, to carry out the thrilling plan He has ordained for your life.

Yet fulfilling your destiny is not automatic. In fact, one of my greatest concerns for people is not that they'll fail in life, but that they'll succeed—in doing the wrong thing. They'll finish the course only to realize they were in the wrong race!

All too often we settle for the canal boat experiences of our past when we could be enjoying the adventures that take place on the railroads and airplanes of God's future. Whether or not you fulfill God's master plan for your life is greatly dependent upon your response to the Holy Spirit's promptings and your willingness to break out of your comfort zones and take faith-filled risks.

The main hindrance to seizing your destiny is the human tendency toward familiarity, comfort and convenience. The Couch Potato Syndrome affects everyone. For millennia the church has battled this tendency, yet in every generation God calls out to those who will wholeheartedly follow the wind of His Spirit and heed His voice to keep advancing.

JESUS *WILL* BUILD HIS CHURCH

Immediately following Peter's confession that Jesus was "the Christ, the Son of the living God," Jesus proclaimed, "I will build my church, and the gates of Hades will not overcome it" (Matt. 16:16, 18).

Throughout the New Testament God unveils His plan to build His church founded upon His Son, Jesus. Someday in the not-too-distant future the church will become a mature, unified body built according to God's plan. (See Ephesians 4:11–13.) It will not be an anemic, compromising, irrelevant organization but rather a "radiant church, without stain or wrinkle or any other blemish, but holy and blameless" (Eph. 5:27).

As a bride, she will "[make] herself ready" (Rev. 19:7)

by heeding the exhortation to "live holy and godly lives as you look forward to the day of God [Jesus' return] and speed its coming" (2 Pet. 3:11–12). Yes, through personal holiness you and I literally can accelerate or delay the return of our Lord. What begins on an individual level with men and women who are committed to holiness becomes corporate-level holiness, which impacts the world. You really do play a part in God's divine drama!

According to Scripture, the Lord's return is dependent upon the whole world hearing the good news of Jesus Christ. In Matthew 24:14, Jesus said, "And this gospel of the kingdom will be preached in the whole world as a testimony to all nations, and then the end will come."

Jesus Christ is not coming back for a beat-up bride! He is returning for dynamic, revolutionary, supernatural men and women who declare and demonstrate the power and passion of the New Testament church. God accomplished His purpose in the first century through one generation, and He is about to do it again!

Before His return, Jesus promised to restore His church and His original intention for humanity (Acts 3:19–21). The true church will be one of power, purity and filled with His presence. Let's look at the activity of God in the lifestyle of the first-century church.

THE EARLY CHURCH DID THE WORKS OF JESUS

The early church was passionate about Jesus. They didn't just go to church once a week, they shared their lives with one another (Acts 2:44–46). They were ablaze with the Holy Spirit's power and regularly experienced supernatural signs and wonders (v. 43). In response to the mighty move of the Holy Spirit, men and women gave their lives to Christ in mass conversions (vv. 41, 47).

Angelic activity was quite common among the early believers. The Book of Acts is not really about the acts of the *apostles*; it's a record of the acts of *the Holy Spirit* in the first forty years of the New Testament church. Surprisingly, it mentions angels a surprising twenty-four times!

In just one chapter—Acts 10—you can read about the following supernatural activities in the first-century church:

- ∽ A heavenly vision (v. 3)
- ∽ Angels speaking (v. 4)
- ∽ A God-given trance (v. 10)
- ∽ People falling under the power of God (v. 25)
- ∽ The outpouring of the Holy Spirit on a group, who then spoke in tongues and praised God (vv. 45–46)

The fledgling church observed God interacting with His people in the following ways:

- ∽ God's direct intervention by slaying two people who lied to the Holy Spirit (Acts 5)
- ∽ God's power throwing an antagonist to the ground (Acts 9:4)
- ∽ God's power striking down an ungodly leader (Acts 12:23)
- ∽ God using an earthquake to free His servants from jail (Acts 16:26)

Spirit-filled believers cast demons out of the lost and pronounced judgment on enemies of the cross (striking one blind in Acts 13:11). God also used His people to raise the dead and, most importantly, to impact entire cities and regions with the gospel of Jesus Christ.

If you were to remove from the Book of Acts every page that mentions a supernatural occurrence, as Thomas Jefferson did in his sanitized version of the Gospels, you would have no pages left. The early church was a holy, dedicated and revolutionary company of committed Christians living life to the hilt for the glory of God. They had their problems (just read 1 and 2 Corinthians), but they were empowered by the Holy Spirit to such a degree that they profoundly impacted their communities for the gospel.

61

THE BOOK OF ACTS IS A DISTURBING BOOK—BUT IT SHOULDN'T BE

J. B. Phillips, in the preface to his translation of the Acts of the Apostles, contrasts the Christian life of the early church with today. You may find what he wrote *disturbing,* just as I did when I first read it:

> It is impossible to spend several months in close study of the remarkable short book, conventionally known as the Acts of the Apostles, without being profoundly stirred and, to be honest, disturbed. The reader is stirred because he is seeing Christianity, the real thing, in action for the first time in human history...Here we are seeing the Church in its first youth, valiant and unspoiled—a body of ordinary men and women bound in an unconquerable fellowship never before seen on this earth.
>
> Yet we cannot help feeling disturbed as well as moved, for this surely is the Church as it was meant to be. It is vigorous and flexible, for these

are the days before it ever became fat and short of breath through prosperity, or muscle bound by over organization. These men did not make "acts of faith," they believed; they did not "say their prayers," they really prayed. They did not hold conferences on psychosomatic medicine, they simply healed the sick. But if they were uncomplicated and naive by modern standards, we have ruefully to admit that they were open on the Godward side in a way that is almost unknown today.

Consequently it is a matter of sober historical fact that never before has any small body of ordinary people so moved the world that their enemies could say, with tears of rage in their eyes, that these men have turned the world upside down (Acts 17:6).

So what happened? Phillips acknowledges that a sincere reading of the Book of Acts is disturbing—but it shouldn't be. One fact is obvious: Until she became legitimized by Emperor Constantine and the Roman government in A.D. 313, the church was vibrant, growing and healthy.

Despite the lukewarmness present among so many Christians, Acts 3:19–21 promises times of refreshing, revival and restoration, eventually culminating in the return of Jesus Christ:

> Repent, then, and turn to God, so that your sins may be wiped out, that times of refreshing may come from the Lord, and that he may send the Christ, who has been appointed for you—even Jesus. He must remain in heaven until the time comes for God to restore everything, as he promised long ago through his holy prophets.

Restoration *will* happen! What you read in the Book of Acts is only a dress rehearsal for the drama that will inevitably culminate with the end of the age. The pattern this passage describes of the early church still remains true today: repentance, revival and then restoration.

God is already creating in this generation a holy dissatisfaction with dead religion and status quo *churchianity*. **Simultaneously He is instilling within the hearts of His people a burning hunger for more of His manifest presence, more of authentic Christianity, simply more of the normative church life found in the early church after Jesus ascended.** 63

A REVIEW OF THE PIONEERING SPIRIT WHO SERVED GOD WITH RECKLESS ABANDON

One of the greatest differences between the New Testament church and most churches today is that the New Testament church was invigorated with God's *conscious* presence. Most churches today are not.

The Bible teaches that there are three aspects of the presence of God. God's *constant* presence is His omnipresence. No place exists where God is not already present—including hell. (See Psalm 139:8; Revelation 14:10.) This constant presence extends to Christians and non-Christians alike.

God's *continuing* presence goes one step further and involves the mysterious presence of Jesus, which occurs among people who know Him. Jesus said, "Where two or three come together in my name, there am I with them"

(Matt. 18:20). He also promised His disciples, "I am with you always" (Matt. 28:20). Through God's continuing presence you receive direction, strength and courage.

God's *conscious* (or manifest, revealed) presence is "God on display." Not only do you believe God is present, or feel it, but you experience it. When Solomon and the priests dedicated the temple, "the priests could not perform their service because of the cloud, for the glory of the LORD filled the temple of God" (2 Chron. 5:14). No one questioned whether or not God was real—they saw the tangible evidence of His presence.

When God poured out His Holy Spirit on the young believers in Acts 2, the people outside heard a rushing wind blowing into the upper room. It was the conscious presence of God. When a non-Christian enters a worship service and hears a word of prophecy that speaks to his heart, Paul says he will "fall down and worship God, exclaiming, 'God is really among you!'" (1 Cor. 14:25).

The New Testament church was immersed in God's conscious presence. Yet over the centuries something changed. How can this be reconciled with what is unfolding today?

Please join me in a brief review of church history. Rather than give you boring, irrelevant dates and facts, I want to take a moment to give you the historical context that explains God's current, ongoing purpose. This is God's drama being played out through the ages. And in each generation He looks for men and women of passion and power who will play a part in His unfolding story.

The names I am about to mention were normal people—just like you and me. Yet their names stand out because of their important contributions to church

64

history as they followed the destinies God had given them. All these people exhibited a discontentment with life as they knew it. At some point each one realized the destiny God had written into the scripts of his or her life, and that individual decided to embark on adventures of which others only dreamed. These people were great—not because they were inherently great, but because they willingly chose to pioneer a new way on God's wild frontier. And you and I need be no different, if we embrace the call of reckless abandon.

65

The record of God's establishing a relationship with His people, of His people drifting, then repenting and of God intervening to revive and restore is the pattern of church history. Keep this thought in mind: "These things happened to them as examples and were written down as warnings for us, on whom the fulfillment of the ages has come" (1 Cor. 10:11).

As we survey the annals of God's people, it is important to remember that *His* story—history—is not one steady, upward progression. Rather it is the account of ups and downs, ebbs and flows, and God's sovereign intervention in revival to accomplish His eternal purpose. One day history will culminate in what Paul describes as a final generation that has "reach[ed] unity in the faith and in the knowledge of the Son of God and become mature, attaining to the whole measure of the fullness of Christ" (Eph. 4:13).

The waves of persecution the early church faced during its first three hundred years served as a fairly effective means of ensuring that people were Christians for the right reasons. However, by the early 300s, a flood of pagans entered the church with heresies and unbiblical customs. Under the Edict of Milan in A.D. 313 *Constantine* and his counterpart in the East, *Emperor Licinius*, granted religious freedom to all beliefs. However, the strongly pro-Christian wording of their edict sent reverberations throughout the Roman Empire.

By A.D. 478—the official date of the fall of Rome— "Christianity" was the prevailing belief in the land. Yet it was a mixture of apostasy and compromise, much as it is today.

The next thousand years are known historically as the Dark Ages of the church. From about A.D. 478 until about A.D. 1500, corruption, greed, favoritism, heresy and spiritual decline characterized the church. Of course, God's truth wasn't entirely abandoned, and His remnant "lights" shined during a period of darkness.

In Ireland, *Patrick* (400s) planted two hundred churches and evangelized over one hundred thousand in only fifteen years. Most amazing of all is that he first arrived in Ireland as a slave and ministered in the country with little or no education!

Francis of Assisi (1200s) was another faithful pioneer who questioned the church's opulence. He called it back to apostolic simplicity and prayed for the pope to be healed of a contagious disease. (He was!) Although he actually was not the author of the famous prayer, "Make me an instrument of Thy peace," he was a radical, spiritual pioneer.

Yet the Dark Ages was largely a period of tragic darkness for the church of Jesus Christ. While avoiding arrogance or a critical spirit, the awful blemishes of church history during this time still must be confronted:

- ∞ Rival popes fought for their "territory" and squelched any dissenters.

- ∞ Courageous, prophetic leaders like *John Huss* (early 1400s) and *Savonarola* (late 1400s) were tortured and burned at the stake for protesting corruption in the church. Others like *John Wycliff* (1300s) and *William Tyndale* (1500s), were persecuted for translating the Scriptures from Latin into the English language.

67

- ∞ Doctrinal errors (such as the sale of indulgences) abounded because the Bible was kept out of the hands of lay people and only interpreted by designated leaders—many of whom held no respect for God and His Word.

- ∞ Misguided, flesh-driven movements such as the Crusades and the Inquisition used force to overcome opposition (from without and within) in order to purify the church. The consequences of these movements linger to this day.

GOD RESTORES THE IMPORTANCE OF SCRIPTURE AND JUSTIFICATION BY FAITH

Despite the corruption and persecution, God used unsuspecting men and women to set the stage for a revival and restoration that reverberates even through today. The simmering volcano finally erupted after approximately one thousand dark years!

First, God planted an idea in the mind of Germany's *Johann Gutenberg* to invent the printing press. The first book he published was the Bible in A.D. 1456. For the first time, the Scriptures could be available to the masses if someone was willing to translate it from Latin into the language of the common person.

On October 31, 1517, an Augustinian monk named *Martin Luther* nailed a document containing ninety-five points of protest to the door of the Castle Church in Wittenberg, Germany, as a basis for debate with church leaders. On All Saints Eve (November 1) a spark was ignited that set the world ablaze!

Luther's "Reformation" spawned other movements throughout Europe founded upon *sola Scriptura* ("Scripture alone") and justification by faith (not by "good works" as the masses had been led to believe).

While hiding from church leaders who were pursuing him, Luther redeemed the time by translating the New Testament into the German vernacular. God was releasing His Word to His people!

Soon other men of God like *John Calvin*, *Ulrich Zwingli* and *John Knox* challenged the status quo as pioneers in their different lands. These and other men compared church practice with the Word of God and chose to venture forward by going back to New Testament church patterns and principles.

As God continued restoring His church, He stirred within the hearts of people like *Conrad Grebel* and *Felix Manz* (both in A.D. 1522) to take them one step further to believer's baptism. These instigators of the Anabaptist movement (*Ana-baptist* means "baptized anew" or "again") rejected infant baptism and taught that baptism followed repentance and faith in Jesus Christ.

It's a sad fact that oftentimes what we learn from history is that we don't learn from history. A new move of God is often most vigorously opposed by those in a former or different move! How important this is to remember today in this transitional time when God is birthing many new and fresh moves, which can seem uncomfortable at first. We can easily cling to the "past move" instead of pressing into the next one.

In Luther's case—you guessed it!—he and many of his followers persecuted the Anabaptists and "urged the use of the sword against them by right of law."[1]

THE NEXT STEP IN RESTORATION: SANCTIFICATION

As time moved on, God continued His reviving and restoring work in His church. During the 1700s God's people recovered the next vital truth in the sequence of restoration—sanctification (practical holiness)—as an essential evidence of genuine conversion.

In England, *John Wesley* (with the help of his brother *Charles Wesley*) pioneered the biblical principle that God calls His people not only to doctrinal purity, but to moral purity also. This five-foot-five-inch firebrand apostle called converts to Christ and sanctified lives in the fire of the Spirit. His apostolic methods of forming "societies" (which many today would consider "cell groups") to foster a holy lifestyle prompted the name "Methodism" and reached hundreds of thousands for Christ.

Many secular historians believe that the revival God worked through the Wesley brothers averted a potential overthrow of the English government—something France was unable to avoid.

Wesley's rallying cry, "Spread scriptural holiness throughout the land!", inspired other men of God like *Jonathan Edwards* and *George Whitefield*, who joined his cause and spawned in England and North America what is now known as the Great Awakening.

EVANGELISM *AND* SOCIAL REFORM
REACH THE MASSES

Next on God's list of priorities was evangelism. Through *William Carey* (A.D. 1761–1834) the modern missions movement was born. His motto, "Expect great things from God; attempt great things for God!", and subsequent successes in India propelled a massive missionary thrust that inspired scores to follow.

Within fifty years of Carey's death, believers in India numbered over half a million! Other missionaries like *David Livingstone* and *Hudson Taylor* (both in the 1800s, one in Africa and the other in China) impacted millions as the "missions building block" was restored and continues to this day.

Two years after John Wesley's death, *Charles Finney* (A.D. 1792–1875) was born. His life linked the First Great Awakening of the 1700s to the Second Great Awakening of the 1800s. This brilliant attorney, who outlived three wives and died at eighty-two, was an instrument of God for revival. Some speculate that as many as half a million people were converted through his ministry—without the benefit of modern transportation and technology.

By the mid-1800s, God began working in His people to merge evangelism with social reform. *General William Booth* and his wife, *Catherine*, founded The Salvation Army in London (their motto: "Soup, Soap and Salvation"). Then in the United States, *D. L. Moody* brought crusade evangelism to new levels while establishing a Bible college and calling the church to minister to the poor.

The mid-1800s also witnessed a backlash of evil on

four fronts as Satan tried to stem God's restoration process:

- ↷ **Karl Marx released** *The Communist Manifesto,* **declaring "the State is god."**

- ↷ **Charles Darwin released his** *Origin of the Species,* **heralding evolution as the explanation for biological creation.**

- ↷ **Sigmund Freud launched his godless psychoanalysis promoting blame-shifting instead of personal responsibility to God.**

- ↷ **Cults like Mormonism, Jehovah's Witnesses and Christian Science were born.**

71

A NEW RELEASE OF THE SPIRIT

To propel His people into the twentieth century, God poured out His Spirit on a humble woman named *Agnes Ozman* in Topeka, Kansas, on the very first day of the new century—New Year's morning 1901! The baptism of the Holy Spirit, evidenced by speaking in other tongues just as the New Testament church experienced in the Book of Acts, was recovered in God's ongoing plan of restoration!

Then on April 9, 1906, the Holy Spirit fell on a small group led by *William Seymour,* a one-eyed, illiterate, African American preacher at the Azusa Street Mission in Los Angeles. From only a handful of hungry folks in a little room on Bonnie Brae Street, God initiated the explosive growth of the Pentecostal/Charismatic movement, which today claims half a billion adherents worldwide! Pentecostal historian Dr. Vinson Synan calls it "by far the largest most important religious movement to originate in the United States."

Out of the fires of the Azusa Street revival, other pioneers restored divine healing to the church. People like *Alexander Dowie, Smith Wigglesworth, John G. Lake, Aimee Semple McPherson, F. F. Bosworth* and later *William Branham* and *Oral Roberts* all pioneered the ministry of supernatural signs and wonders so long missing from the church.

At the same time, gifted teachers like *A. W. Tozer* and *Gordon Lindsey* helped bring balance to this new outpouring of the Spirit through their writing. The same night that former baseball star turned evangelist *Billy Sunday* died (1935), God saved a young man at a tent meeting named *William Franklin Graham.* Billy Graham went on to preach the gospel to over 200 million people—more than any person in history!

Between 1948 and 1957, the Latter Rain movement quickly spread from its base in Canada into the United States and into other countries of the world. God used it to restore biblical truths to His people regarding prophecy, the ministry of laying on of hands, free-flowing worship in Spirit and truth and insights concerning church order and government. The Latter Rain revival influenced millions even though it was brief in duration and unfortunately veered off track due to a lack of seasoned, apostolic leadership.

The late sixties and early seventies ushered in a fresh move of God's Spirit on numerous fronts:

∾**The Jesus People movement, led by *Chuck Smith* of Calvary Chapel and others, swept countless thousands of** hippies and disillusioned youth into God's kingdom and launched a new breed of churches and music.

∞ The Charismatic Renewal became a widespread phenomenon as millions of people among the historic, mainline denominations were baptized in the Spirit and ushered into new life (myself included!).

∞ Through the Messianic Jewish movement, God began drawing His chosen people back to Himself. *Moishe Rosen* of Jews for Jesus was one of many leaders who proclaimed that one could be both a Jew and a Messianic believer.

∞ Last of all, the Word of Faith movement taught Christians how to live as overcomers in the fullness of God's provision. *Kenneth Hagin* was a true pioneer and father of this new emphasis on faith, and he discipled other leaders like *Kenneth Copeland* and *Fred Price.* In spite of some understandable mistakes and misunderstandings associated with the Faith movement, God used and continues to use this teaching to transform millions of lives from defeat to victory.

In recent years God has used different forms of media to deliver new wine to His people. *Charisma* magazine communicates the Holy Spirit's activity around the world. Integrity's Hosanna! music and other companies disseminate the power of anointed praise and worship. Satellites now enable people to receive anointed teaching through the Trinity Broadcasting Network (TBN) and other networks.

Most recently, God has used the revivals in Toronto, Ontario and Pensacola, Florida (the Brownsville Revival) to profoundly touch millions of lives with the power of God.

REVIVAL BEGINS WITH ONLY ONE PERSON

But consider this: God launched the entire Pentecostal/Charismatic movement (which grew from one person to half a billion adherents in only one hundred years) by pouring out His Spirit on one person—*Agnes Ozman*. One person!

Henry Varley, a British revivalist, befriended young D. L. Moody in 1873 and challenged him with these words: "The world has yet to see what God can do with, for and in the man fully consecrated to Him."

"By God's help," Moody answered, "I will be that man."

Varley's words serve as a challenge even today. The world still hasn't seen what God can do with a man—or woman—fully consecrated to Him. But looking back through history proves that Jesus is truly building His church. And the pillars of that church are the spiritual pioneers—the men and women who make full consecration to God their aim. The pillars of His church are men and women who believe that God has a destiny for their lives and with reckless abandon pursue it.

My friend, you are no different. God has a destiny for you that is limited only by your faith to believe and your resolve to be fully consecrated to Him. Do you aim to be that man or woman? If you do, then be prepared for God to use YOU to help change history and participate in the revival and restoration of His church!

Five

Jesus—or Just an Imitation?

Imagine traversing the vast Midwestern prairies in a covered wagon. As you roll along, in the distance you notice a row of bumps slowly rising from the plains. As you continue traveling west, the bumps slowly grow into hills, and the hills eventually become the Rocky Mountains.

How are you going to get over the mountains in your covered wagon? And how long will it take until you reach level ground again? No road signs or interstate highways exist to help guide you through. You have no idea how long it will take to get across, but this you know: If you get caught in the mountains during the winter, you *will* die.

Yet somehow, pioneers risked all they owned—even their very lives—to conquer the mountains and deserts that stood before them.

The pioneers who ventured west two centuries ago left behind their friends, extended families and their lives of security because they were consumed by a singular passion. To some it was land for farming. To some it was gold or silver, and to others it was the quest for religious freedom. Without that driving passion, these early pioneers would quickly have given up at the first sign of trouble.

What is *your* passion? What drives you to scale the mountains that stand in your way? Is it fame? Wealth? Success? Respect? Your passion not only reveals your heart, but it also determines the destination you will someday hopefully reach. How you respond to obstacles you encounter along the way surfaces your true passion and how deeply you hold it.

76

MISGUIDED PASSION—NO MATTER HOW WELL-INTENTIONED—IS STILL MISGUIDED

Through the obstacles I faced, God revealed my own misguided passions. He jolted me as one of my children began deviating from the "straight and narrow." He stripped me and broke me by removing all my props— security, reputation, position. He brought me to the end of myself where all I seemingly had left, apart from my family and a few loyal friends, was Him.

Was this a satanic attack? No. God orchestrated these events in my life so I could see the waywardness of my own heart. He had me right where He wanted me. Even the sincere yet, in part, misguided efforts of some long-standing friends were used to accomplish His will for my life.

King Solomon once wrote, "Faithful are the wounds of a friend" (Prov. 27:6, NAS). Sometimes we need to hear a hard word—a word that wounds—and we will only hear it if it comes from a close friend. When my heart was finally open to hearing His faithful words, God spoke to me through a sermon I had preached years earlier. While listening to an old sermon tape, I heard these words come from my mouth: "What is the purpose of God in our generation? What is on God's heart as priority number one? It's passion for the church!"

In that moment, God made painfully clear to me that I had subtly veered away from His true purpose, His number one priority—it was not *passion for the church*, it was *passion for Jesus*. I had wrongly made the body of Christ my focus rather than Jesus Himself.

God wasn't calling me to forsake the church (of course!). He was calling me back to Himself—to recover my first love for Jesus Christ and to enjoy ongoing, ever-deepening fellowship and friendship with Him. From there He could redirect my path as a pioneer for the next step on His agenda. The subtle error had to be corrected. God was calling me and the people I would lead back to intimacy with Him.

> I am jealous for you with a godly jealousy. I promised you to one husband, to Christ, so that I might present you as a pure virgin to him. But I am afraid that just as Eve was deceived by the serpent's cunning, your minds may somehow be led astray from your sincere and pure devotion to Christ.
> —2 CORINTHIANS 11:2–3

As I transitioned out of one ministry season to the next, I began to position myself daily on my knees in the privacy of my living room to worship God. As I sang to the Lord in the emptiness of that room I felt God drawing me back to a sincere and pure devotion to Jesus.

WILL THE REAL JESUS PLEASE STAND UP?

Years ago at Harvard University, the following message was scrawled in chalk on an aged wall:

> Who do men say that I am?
>
> Thou art the eschatological manifestation of the ground of our being; the ultimate Kerygma in whom we find the profound solution to our mystical inner quest.
>
> And Jesus replied: "What!?"

The question Jesus posed to His disciples in Matthew 16 is just as important today as it was two thousand years ago: "Who do you say that I am?"

Not long ago, if you were to ask nearly any person in North America, "Who is Jesus?", you would likely hear the reply, "The Son of God." Whether or not during that time people chose to follow the Son of God was an entirely different issue. But suffice it to say that society held a basic concept of who Jesus was.

Evangelists like George Whitefield and Charles Finney (whom I mentioned in the last chapter) didn't have to argue the existence of God. They merely preached to the masses about the lordship of Jesus—who the people already knew existed—much as they would in a church service.

MANY PEOPLE REJECT A CARICATURE OF JESUS

Today, however, we live in a society that is suffering from a "Jesus identity crisis." How do your neighbors (or even you, possibly) view Jesus? In my experience, I have found that for many people, the person of Jesus Christ conjures up images of a poker-faced, wimpy, somewhat strange type of bearded killjoy who never smiled, always appeared somewhat emaciated and had chubby little cherubs floating about his head. This is the meek, mild, milquetoast image of Jesus imbedded in many people's minds. What a distortion of the true Son of God!

Most of the people you and I are trying to reach with the gospel have major misconceptions concerning the person of Jesus Christ for several reasons: no religious background, faulty religious training or misrepresentations of biblical truth popularized in the media.

A brief look at how the movies have portrayed Jesus only confirms this idea:

> ∞ In the film *The Greatest Story Ever Told,* Max von Sydow portrays an aloof, bland, expressionless, glum, stain-glassed, Prozac Jesus who seemingly floats around devoid of emotion and substance.

> ∞ Musicals like *Jesus Christ Superstar* and *Godspell* present a super guru Savior and conclude with Jesus' death—but no resurrection! In the former, Jesus angrily confronts His heavenly Father at Gethsemane in a state of resignation and confusion, finally consenting to die. Meanwhile Mary Magdalene tells the audience, "He's a man; He's just a man."

∽The controversial movie *The Last Temptation of Christ* presents a dream sequence showing Jesus involved sexually with a woman! On a no-less-offensive note, *The Gospel According to St. Matthew* depicts Jesus as a humorless radical.

Satan's mission is to distort the image of the real Jesus, to keep people from finding fascination in the Son of God. My friend Mike Bickle says, "Most people think of Jesus as mainly sad and mainly mad but rarely glad!"

MANY PEOPLE ALSO REJECT A CARICATURE OF CHRISTIANS

Now if non-Christians believe what many of the movies say about *Jesus*—that He was mainly sad and mainly mad but rarely glad—then they may also assume that *Christians* also are mainly sad and mainly mad but rarely glad.

The prevailing perception of a Christian in modern society is of one who is slightly out-of-touch, intellectually weak (why else would you need a religious "crutch"?), a bit homely, given to drab clothing and outdated hairstyles, enslaved by a long list of dos and don'ts...someone who, in a word, is "weird." The media often promotes this image through negative portrayals of ministers who are sexually immoral charlatans. Popular descriptions of Christians include "fundamentalist," "religious right" or "anti-abortionist."

Although you and I may bristle at the caricature thrust upon us, from where do you think the misrepresentation came? It came from Christians like you and me!

The pressure to conform to the world's standard of behavior, which includes approval of premarital sex, abortion, divorce and homosexuality, is strong. However, the way many Christians resist it reinforces the notion that Christians are negative people who are against just about everything.

While it's true that genuine followers of Jesus Christ should be opposed to abortion, premarital sex, homo-sexuality and other forms of self-indulgent behavior, the focus of your life should be primarily *positive*, not negative:

81

 → You may oppose abortion, but you can stress to others the sanctity of human life and compassionate care for the unborn, elderly and handicapped.

 → You may be against sex outside of marriage, but you can accentuate the rich and fulfilling sexual relationship that results from the security of the marriage covenant.

 → You may object to homosexual behavior, yet you can extol the value that comes from healthy friendships and godly displays of affection.

 → You may disapprove of drunkenness, recreational drugs and self-indulgent "partying," but you can celebrate and enjoy life in wholesome fellowship, hospitality and recreation.

You can obliterate the caricature people have of Christians by entering into and demonstrating a dynamic relationship with the living Son of God who brings joy and freedom. Remember that Christianity isn't a *religion***; it's a** *relationship***.**

Often when I'm out for a time of fellowship with some of my ministry colleagues, I enjoy posing a question to our waitress who has observed our friendship and spontaneous fun.

"'Scuse me, Kathy. Can I ask you a question before we leave?"

"Uh...yeah..."

"You've waited on our table tonight, and you've done a great job. As you've seen us interact, what do you think we do? We're all in the same line of work."

Usually taken aback, yet enjoying the challenge, waitresses over the years have said:

82

"Are you a basketball team?"

"You guys play rugby?"

"You all sell Amway!"

"You're actors?"

How refreshing it is to watch the lady's expression as I relate our diverse backgrounds and tie it all together through our common commitment to Jesus and work as pastors.

Somehow it doesn't compute. "But I thought pastors were...wore...talked like..."

Handing her my personal testimony tract (along with a generous tip), I believe we've drawn another person in this generation a little bit further from misconception and a little bit closer to the real Jesus.

MANY PEOPLE ALSO REJECT A CARICATURE OF THE CHURCH!

In the same way that many people in society accept misconceptions about Jesus and Christians, they also accept misconceptions about the church.

Try taking a poll in your community by asking the following question: "What comes to mind when I say the word *church*?" You will likely hear the following descriptions:

ca "It's boring."

ca "A waste of time."

ca "Irrelevant...at least that's what it was like for me."

Although an increasing number of people have no experience whatsoever with the church, others who no longer attend only remember the cold, antiseptic, library atmospheres of their past. There, everyone sat politely on hard, wooden pews listening to a man talk in a monotone voice about matters they didn't under- *83* stand. All the while, people kept glancing at their watches to see how much longer they'd have to endure.

Of course, this is a generalization. Many churches *did* impact lives for the gospel in the past. But for millions of poor souls, little positive impact remains.

But we also have to admit that although the caricatures our society holds of Jesus, Christians and the church may be untrue, they contain a shred of truth. These caricatures exist because many Christians have a faulty view of Jesus.

How you see Jesus affects not only the way you live as a Christian; it also affects the way we all act when we get together— as a church. As the body of Christ, our actions represent—or misrepresent—Jesus.

If this generation is going to be reached for the gospel, then many Christians' understanding of Jesus and the church needs to be changed. The church is not a building. It is a community of people who love Jesus passionately, who celebrate God's mercy and grace and who love to splash in the river of the Holy Spirit.

When you invite unbelieving guests to church, they should encounter warm, friendly people who know that

Christianity is not merely a Sunday service to attend—
but rather it's a life to share. In this atmosphere of
warmth and acceptance, your friends should hear
preaching that is anointed, sincere and relevant to their
needs—at home and in the workplace. The worship
they encounter should pulsate with life and meaning,
and it should be expressed in the language and music
styles of their culture. But most of all, the people they
meet should be passionately in love with Jesus.

If every church were committed to this picture, you
would witness the greatest spiritual harvest in history!

Unfortunately, Satan has succeeded masterfully in
presenting a counterfeit Christ not only to the secular
culture but to Christians as well. Just as I had to do a
few years ago, you may need to see Jesus with new
eyes.

**Right thinking breeds right behavior. If
you understand who the real Jesus is,
and if you engage in a relationship with
Him, you will be changed, as will your
church. So, who is this Jesus we love,
honor, worship and follow? Who is He...
really? We'll seek for the answers to
those questions in the next chapter.**

84

Six

How to Know the Real Jesus

During the nineteenth century, liberal theologians began a search to rediscover the historical Jesus. They were intent on determining the true personality of a Jesus who existed two thousand years earlier. Leading this pursuit was Dr. Albert Schweitzer, the Nobel Peace Prize-winning philosopher, theologian and medical missionary. The fruit of his work was disclosed in his highly acclaimed book *The Quest of the Historical Jesus*, which was released in 1906—the same year the Azusa Street revival lit the world on fire.

After exhaustive research, Schweitzer concluded that Jesus was a mysterious, power-hungry ruler who arrogantly considered Himself the Son of Man. Titles like *Messiah, Son of Man* and *Son of God* were merely "historical parables." In other words, Jesus' claims of divinity were not based in reality. Schweitzer concluded, "We can find no designation that expresses what He is for us."[1]

In Schweitzer's opinion, Jesus was a mysterious man

who had nothing in common with contemporary society, but could be known in some way through individual experience. For Schweitzer that meant running a hospital in Africa. Although he helped a great deal of people and was truly sincere—this misguided pioneer was sincerely wrong.

Schweitzer sought the Jesus of two thousand years ago rather than the Jesus of today. The tools of his research were human intellect, the scientific method and subjective experience rather than Scripture, prayer and meditation.

How important is it to rediscover the Jesus of the Bible? I venture to say it means everything. However, revelation—which doesn't come from human intellect or the scientific method—is at the core of who Jesus is. Revelation is the process God uses to show the beauty and power of Jesus in your life through the Word of God.

Nearly thirty years after Jesus' death and resurrection, Paul wrote, "I want to know Christ and the power of his resurrection and the fellowship of sharing in his sufferings" (Phil. 3:10). When you know the Jesus of the Bible, you daily fall more and more in love with Him.

Jesus doesn't want you following Him out of cold, rigid, legalistic obedience as if He were an impersonal taskmaster or an exacting judge. He desires to relate to you not as some distant, mysterious Supreme Being, but in the warm context of a Bridegroom with His bride. He wants you "running the race" right beside Him, on His team. And He wants you to obey Him because you love Him and delight in pleasing Him!

Yes, He is a monarch and righteous ruler, but He is foremost a loving Lord

86

who laid down His life for you and continues to pray for you every day before the Father (Heb. 7:25).

Jesus wants you captivated, fascinated and exhilarated by a true revelation of Him instead of old, stale religion (which rarely attracts anyone).

The only definition in the Bible for *eternal life* is found in the high-priestly prayer of our Lord Jesus prior to His crucifixion. He prayed, "Now this is eternal life: that they may know you, the only true God, and Jesus Christ, whom you have sent" (John 17:3).

87

The concept behind "knowing" in Scripture is not academic acceptance of facts but rather intimate, experiential relationship. Albert Schweitzer sought to know the historical Jesus through human experience. Pioneers, on the other hand, seek to know the biblical Jesus in the human experience.

The classic Westminster Catechism put it this way: "The chief end of man is to know God and enjoy Him forever." You know and enjoy God through a personal relationship with Jesus Christ.

In the closing hours of her life, Eileen Wallis (wife of one of England's premier pioneers and prophets, Arthur Wallis) gave me this counsel: "Enjoy Jesus, Larry. Take time to simply enjoy being with Him." The reason for studying God (theology) is not primarily for information, but rather for revelation (knowing Him for who He really is) and transformation (becoming more like Him). We must keep the main thing, the main thing—knowing God accurately and enjoying Him personally.

You Can Only Know Jesus Through the Bible

Both Albert Schweitzer and I experienced misguided attempts at knowing Jesus. I sought to know Jesus in the present solely through a past revelation of Him. Schweitzer simply sought to know the historical Jesus of the past. Either way, our searches were for the person of Jesus. But only through a *biblical* revelation of the person of Jesus in the present can you truly know Him.

88

To know Jesus, you must first begin with the Bible. Jesus said, "You diligently study the Scriptures because you think that by them you possess eternal life. These are the Scriptures that testify about me, yet you refuse to come to me to have life" (John 5:39). On the road to Emmaus after Jesus rose from the dead, it is recorded: "And beginning with Moses and all the Prophets, he explained to them what was said in all the Scriptures concerning himself" (Luke 24:27).

The Bible was written to introduce you to a Person— Jesus. And by wholeheartedly believing in Him, you can share eternity with Him. In the closing words of his Gospel, John wrote, "But these are written that you may believe that Jesus is the Christ, the Son of God, and that by believing you may have life in his name" (John 20:31).

C. S. Lewis said it best: "We come to Scripture not to learn a subject but to steep ourselves in a Person."

For many Christians, believing in Jesus the Son of God is much easier than believing in Jesus the Son of Man—a real, live person. Without forfeiting any of His divinity, Jesus came to earth and clothed Himself with human skin. Philippians 2 describes Jesus as "being made in human likeness" and having the "appearance as a man" (vv. 7–8).

But after His resurrection, Jesus didn't stop being a man. The apostle Paul wrote, "For there is one God and one Mediator between God and men, the *man Christ Jesus*" (1 Tim. 2:5, emphasis added). The man Christ Jesus was your mediator two thousand years ago when He died for your sins, and He is your mediator right now.

Jesus did not temporarily become a man (the incarnation) for a season and then return to heaven, dissolve His humanity and "go back to being only God." The eternal, uncreated, omnipotent, omniscient, omnipresent second Person of the Trinity became a man and will remain a man forever!

89

Relating to a personal God who is a literal person is so much easier than relating to some "beatific vision" or "ethereal presence" or, pardon the expression, to simply "let the Force be with you." Unfortunately, a great deal of religious training not only distorts the personality of Jesus but also ignores His humanity in attempting to emphasize His divinity. We need both!

The tendency among Christians is to overemphasize Jesus' divinity. Among non-Christians, the tendency is to overemphasize Jesus' humanity (for obvious reasons). But by building a friendship with the man Christ Jesus, you build a relationship with Jesus, the Son of God.

During the 1870s two unbelievers sat on a railroad train discussing the life of Christ. Both were skeptical attorneys, one a writer, one a famous agnostic. "I think an interesting romance could be written about Him," the writer commented.

His friend replied, "And you are just the man to write it. Tear down the prevailing sentiment about His divinity and paint Him as a man."

The writer, former Civil War general Lewis Wallace, accepted his friend's challenge. Yet the challenge didn't come from an unknown agnostic attorney. It came from a noted opponent of Christianity, Robert Ingersoll, whose scurrilous attacks on biblical belief commanded up to $3,500 for one lecture (a hefty sum in those days).

In the process of constructing the history of Christ, Wallace found himself facing the greatest life ever lived on earth. The more he studied the Bible, the more he was convinced. He fell in love with the compassionate Savior. His heart was captured until, one day, he felt compelled to cry, "Truly this was the Son of God."

He finished the book, too. It eventually became the all-time classic *Ben Hur*.

MEET THE REAL JESUS!

The apostle Paul knew the real Jesus, and his ardent desire was to share his passion for Jesus with others. He wrote:

> I pray that you, being rooted and established in love, may have power, together with all the saints, to grasp how wide and long and high and deep is the love of Christ, and to know this love that surpasses knowledge—that you may be filled to the measure of all the fullness of God.
> —EPHESIANS 3:17–19

God wants you to know the love of Christ, which surpasses knowledge. He wants you to drink deeply of His love and discover the beauty, the reality of His only begotten Son who is "beautiful beyond description." The real Jesus is full of life and joy, and He loves you extravagantly. In fact, Scripture says He not only saves you, but He also sings over you!

> On that day they will say to Jerusalem, "Do not fear, O Zion; do not let your hands hang limp. The LORD your God is with you, he is mighty to save. He will take great delight in you, he will quiet you with his love, he will rejoice over you with singing."
>
> —ZEPHANIAH 3:16–17

91

God is more than an impersonal Being who is angry at you, or who merely tolerates you or views you primarily as a struggling sinner. The Bible says that God loves you and delights in you so much that in spite of your shortcomings and sins He bursts forth in heartfelt song! If you are a Christian, the wrath of God is no longer upon you...He's not mad at you anymore... He's on your side!

Believe it or not, God enjoys you. He not only loves you, but He likes you too, and He wants to spend time with you, sharing His secrets with you on your pilgrimage. He wants you to follow Him out of sheer delight, captivated by the compelling personality and character of His one and only Son.

THE SPIRIT AND THE BRIDE SAY, "COME!"

Fueling the pioneer's drive to continue forward over every obstacle that stands in the way is the revelation of the divine romance of the Bridegroom and His bride. It's true that love knows no distance—true love crosses any barrier and any border to be united with its lover.

> The Spirit and the bride say, "Come!" And let him who hears say, "Come!" Whoever is thirsty, let him come; and whoever wishes, let him take the free gift of the water of life.
>
> —REVELATION 22:17

In the deep recesses of every heart, Jesus whispers, "Come. Stop trying to fill the hole in your heart with things that cannot satisfy. Drink of My love and find true life." A love relationship with Jesus is the foundation of your very life.

Jesus is the Bridegroom who ravishes His bride, the church, with His love. This same Jesus ravishes you with His love. Jesus wants a full-time bride—not some part-time girlfriend! To see yourself as part of a bridal company is not about *gender* but *position*—He longs to be with you as a bridegroom does with his bride! It is this joyful Jesus who, as a bridegroom, beckons you to follow Him as His beloved bride on the path of a pioneer.

The twenty-first-century pioneer is eager to respond to the winsome call of a joyful Jesus who said, "These things I have spoken to you, that My joy may be in you, and that your joy may be made full" (John 15:11, NAS).

Who is this person who calls you to Himself? It's the festive Jesus who enjoys celebrating a wedding feast; the servant Jesus who prepares a seaside breakfast for His men; the masculine Jesus whom brawny fishermen follow unashamedly. It is the pure Jesus whom hypocritical leaders despise, and the joyful Jesus whose infectious smile melts the hearts of multitudes. The mere presence of this Jesus (while still in the womb!) brings joy. (See Luke 1:44.)

THIS IS THE JESUS OF MY FIRST LOVE   93

The Jesus I am describing is the Jesus who won my heart when I was much younger. After twenty years of emptiness, which included twelve years of religious schooling, as a young man I discovered that true Christianity is not based on religious rules. It is based on a living, dynamic relationship with Jesus Christ.

Up to that point in my life I had searched everywhere for peace and purpose. But then someone introduced me to Jesus. Scales lifted from my eyes, and I realized that Christianity was not about performance or production—it was about a Person! I was overwhelmed by the real Jesus of the Bible, and I embraced a relationship with the One who created me and laid down His life for me so I could experience His abundant life. (See John 10:10.)

Over time, however, I strayed from my love relationship with Jesus. The tendency after experiencing a true revelation of Him is to replace intimacy with ministry, passion for the Lord of the work with production for the work of the Lord. At one time I enjoyed walking with Him in the "cool of the day"; then I endured working for Him in the crunch of the deadline. While Jesus was calling me back to emulating Mary, I was stuck mimicking Martha. (See Luke 10:38–42.) I needed to discover Jesus again. I needed to leap off the treadmill of performance and pressure, back into the loving arms of the smiling Shepherd I once knew.

How about you? Are you enjoying your relationship with Jesus Christ, or have you slipped from sheer delight in Him to drudgery, activity and more and more ministry?

If your hunger to spend time communing with Jesus has decreased, if your experiences of God's faithfulness are limited to stories in the past or if you struggle continually to win the victory over the battles that stand in your way, you may need to rediscover Jesus, too. These are all symptoms of a heart grown cold.

Jesus spoke to a group of believers who became settled in their relationship with Him. In Revelation 2, Jesus spoke to the church of Ephesus:

> I know your deeds, your hard work and your perseverance. I know that you cannot tolerate wicked men, that you have tested those who claim to be apostles but are not, and have found them false. You have persevered and have endured hardships for my name, and have not grown weary. Yet I hold this against you: You have forsaken your first love.
> —REVELATION 2:2–4

The Christians in Ephesus weren't bad people. They opposed wickedness; they tested all teaching with the truth of God's Word; and they refused to give up under persecution. From the outward appearance, these people would be considered solid Christians—and they were. Yet, Jesus said, "You have forsaken your first love."

In order to move forward as spiritual pioneers, Jesus gave them these instructions: "Remember the height from that you have fallen! Repent and do the things you did at first" (Rev. 2:5).

If you can identify with these solid believers, then this scripture gives three simple keys that will help rekindle your passion for Jesus.

95

∞ *Remember*—**Think back to the former days when you enjoyed the sweetness of Jesus' presence and favor.**

∞ *Repent*—**In prayer, confess that you have allowed yourself to stray from your first love. Ask for forgiveness, and choose to turn around and return to Jesus.**

∞ *Repeat*—**Do again those simple things you did to cultivate your relationship with Jesus. Read your Bible, and spend consistent quality time with Him in worship, prayer and meditation. Remember He likes you, He longs for you—in spite of your shortcomings and sin.**

Respond to His calling you as His bride, motivated not by guilt and pressure but rather by His deep-seated, passionate devotion to you! "We love [him] because he first loved us" (1 John 4:19). What a joy it is to rediscover Jesus and be rekindled in bridal affection for Him as the "lover of our soul."

Seven

True Revival

Throughout history, when the church has lost or at least misplaced her first love for Jesus, God has stirred the hearts of individuals to return to Him and then pray for revival. These spiritual pioneers refuse to be disheartened by the prevailing sentiment of their time. Instead, as they are renewed in their relationship with Him, they then forge ahead in prayer, petitioning the Father to awaken His people through revival.

Spiritual pioneers seek an ongoing reviving of the church because they know that revival is God's historical way of arousing a slumbering people back to Himself and His purposes.

A leader once commented to me over lunch that the Brownsville revival in Pensacola, Florida was something God decided to do because "He is sovereign." While it is true that God is sovereign—He has the ultimate power to choose and carry out His will—His omnipotence does not absolve His people from the responsibility to fast and pray.

God promises, "If my people, who are called by my name, will humble themselves and pray and seek my face and turn from their wicked ways, then will I hear from heaven and will forgive their sin and will heal their land" (2 Chron. 7:14).

When the people of God appeal to Him in humility, repentance and unwavering prayer, He honors their request and opens the floodgates of heaven in a downpour of His Spirit. The Brownsville revival, in fact, was preceded by over two years of unwavering, passionate prayer.

REVIVAL BEGINS WITH PRAYERFUL PEOPLE

97

Revivals date back to Bible times. Men like David, Hezekiah, Josiah, Ezra and Nehemiah were instrumental in spurring new awakenings in their generations. Scripture is filled with the prayers of people like you and me who desperately sought God for a fresh touch in their generation. Read these brief prayers from the Bible, and let them become your prayer, too:

Asaph, a worship leader for King David, prayed:

> Let your hand rest on the man at your right hand, the son of man you have raised up for yourself. Then we will not turn away from you; revive us, and we will call on your name. Restore us, O LORD God Almighty; make your face shine upon us, that we may be saved.
>
> —PSALM 80:17–19

The Sons of Korah, a choir that ministered in the courts of David, implored God:

> Will you not revive us again, that your people may
> rejoice in you?
> —PSALM 85:6

The prophet Isaiah sought God on behalf of his
people:

> Oh, that you would rend the heavens and come
> down, that the mountains would tremble before
> you! As when fire sets twigs ablaze and causes
> water to boil, come down to make your name
> known to your enemies and cause the nations to
> quake before you! For when you did awesome
> things that we did not expect, you came down, and
> the mountains trembled before you.
> —ISAIAH 64:1–3

At a time when his people were beginning to suffer
judgment and the consequences of their sins, the
prophet Habakkuk implored God:

> LORD, I have heard of your fame; I stand in awe of
> your deeds, O LORD. Renew them in our day, in our
> time make them known; in wrath remember mercy.
> —HABAKKUK 3:2

Of course, the most well-known outpouring of the
Holy Spirit occurred at Pentecost (in Acts 2), spawning
the birth of the church. Incidentally, that particular
revival was preceded by forty days of passionate, con-
certed prayer.

Periods of renewal and revival were sporadic until the
Reformation of the 1500s (which I dealt with in chapter
four). Since then, the "birth pangs" have increased in
frequency and intensity—especially in the last one
hundred years.

The twentieth century alone experienced, among others, the 1904 Welsh revival (Evan Roberts), the 1906 Azuza Street revival (William Seymour), the 1948 Hebrides revival (Duncan Campbell) and the Argentine (Carlos Annacondia) and Pensacola (John Kilpatrick, Steve Hill and Dr. Michael Brown) revivals near the end of the twentieth century.

You may notice that I have included the names of individuals who were instrumental in these moves of God. I do so because God chooses to pour out His Spirit through *people*. If you choose to follow Jesus Christ with reckless abandon and seek Him with your whole heart in prayer, He could spawn the next great move of God through consecrated Christians like *you and me!* With reckless abandon, let's respond to the trumpet call.

99

REVIVAL IS THE RESTORATION OF THE NEW TESTAMENT CHURCH

So what, then, is *revival*? As you can tell from the prayers you just read, revival is not a series of scheduled meetings, a mass evangelistic crusade or an outbreak of emotional fervor. Neither is it something you can "work up." Rather, it is something God sends down!

Revival **is an extraordinary move of the Holy Spirit that produces extraordinary results. The word** *revival* **literally means, "to make alive again."**

Revival historian J. Edwin Orr once explained revival as "a movement of the Holy Spirit bringing about a reviving of New Testament Christianity in the church and its related community." Revival, then, is the restoration of the church to New Testament Christianity.

Just as God broke through to a first-century generation characterized by dead religion and compromise, so
too is He breaking through the dead religion and compromise of today. God's Holy Spirit is being poured out
in response to the passionate prayers of His people. And,
as a result, the New Testament church of the Book of
Acts is being restored. You are living in an historic hour!

Here is a snapshot of how the New Testament church
described the revival that was taking place in that day:

Shortly after Pentecost, Peter and John were going to
the temple to pray (see again the relationship between
revival and prayer?) when they encountered a crippled
beggar sitting at the gate. Although they had no money
to give him, they gave him something much better—
new legs! Peter pulled him to his feet, and the healed
man began jumping and praising God. The commotion
going on at the front of the temple attracted a crowd—
in fact, people began running toward them from all
around. They wanted what the healed man had!

Never one to miss an opportunity to share good news
of Jesus Christ, Peter explained to the onlookers how
they could receive a touch as well:

> Repent, then, and turn to God, so that your sins
> may be wiped out, that times of *refreshing* may
> come from the Lord, and that he may send the
> Christ, who has been appointed for you—even
> Jesus. He must remain in heaven until the time
> comes for God to *restore* everything, as he promised
> long ago through his holy prophets.
> —ACTS 3:19–21, EMPHASIS ADDED

Two words in this passage describe the way God works

through revival. The first word is *refresh*. The Greek word for *refresh* means "cooling, relief, rest, or even to take one's breath."[1] It is the release from tiredness and discouragement, from inhibition and fear. When you are refreshed by the Holy Spirit, you feel energized and eager to serve God. The phrase "times of refreshing" indicates that you can expect such seasons again and again.

The second word Peter uses in this passage is *restore*, which means, "to return to an original condition." The work of the Holy Spirit is to return people not only back to the New Testament church, but even further back to the period before the fall of Adam and Eve. God seeks to restore us, His church, and ultimately the world, to a place of purity and unhindered relationship with Him. From the beginning, God's intention was to prepare a bride for His Son. That bride is the church in a place of beauty, purity and intimacy—displayed before a watching world.

As you have been reading, you may have noticed that despite moving forward, true pioneers of the Spirit are people who also move backward. They seek the restoration of the New Testament church in their generation, but realize they can only go back by moving ahead with the Spirit.

God Sends Revival Not for Our Sake, but for His

Why does God send His presence and power through revival? He doesn't do it for us—He does it for Himself. God sends revival fire when His people have strayed (like today) in order to restore the glory of His holy name!

During a period of compromise in Israel's past, God

spoke through the prophet Ezekiel:

> It is not for your sake, O house of Israel, that I am going to do these things, but for the sake of my holy name... Then the nations will know that I am the LORD, declares the Sovereign LORD, when I show myself holy through you before their eyes.
> —EZEKIEL 36:22–23

So if God sends revival for His sake and not the church's, *why has God taken so long to send revival, and why isn't there more of it?* It's because God refuses to send revival when people are content to live without it!

But in recent days, God has been instilling in the hearts of His people a discontentment with "the same old, same old" lifeless, predictable, worship services. He's raising up pioneers who are taking their brothers and sisters in Christ past the shallow sermonettes and silly, peppy, man-centered choruses that dilute New Testament Christianity. And He's stirring people to earnestly pray for more of God.

True Christianity is not about more bodies, bucks and buildings; it's about people like you and me who hunger and thirst for more of God. It's about men and women who are desperate and broken and who realize that the best church programs, the best sermons, the best conferences cannot substitute for a supernatural visitation of the Holy Spirit. Only then will the church rise again in purity, power and passion for the glory of God. Only then will we represent a true threat to the kingdom of darkness and make a difference in our day.

If ever a heaven-sent revival was needed, it is today! A revival is necessary to counteract spiritual decline and to create

spiritual momentum. A revival is necessary to shake up the status quo of slumbering saints and complacent churches. A revival is necessary to reach the next generation, which is leaving dead religion in droves.

YOU CAN EXPERIENCE REVIVAL WITHOUT BEING EXTREME

Navigating your way through revival waters, though, can be a risky venture. Because Satan is an extremist, he will do anything he can to lure you to either end of the spectrum. He wants you to become skeptical and to misunderstand what revival really is. Or he wants you to base it entirely upon your emotions.

103

Every move of the Spirit is always accompanied by responses in the flesh. Just because unbiblical, fleshly responses are present doesn't necessarily mean that you should "throw out the baby with the bath water." But neither do you have to "drink the dirty bath water!" That is why strong apostolic leaders are needed—to help keep people on the right track.

You cannot be a twenty-first-century pioneer and play it safe at the same time. If you insist on remaining in your comfort zone, you will *miss* what God intends to work in your life. The key is to focus your eyes on the Word of God while attuning your spiritual ears to the Holy Spirit. If you do both, the Holy Spirit will keep you on track.

Not long ago I spoke with a friend in another city who is a member of a large church that emphasizes uncompromising orthodoxy (doctrinal correctness). People in this church who yearn for their congregation to network with other Christian churches and ministries that may vary on minor points of doctrine are viewed by the leadership as too "eclectic" or "undiscerning." Due to past abuses of previous moves of God (the flesh that often accompanies moves of the Spirit), the leadership holds a cautionary stance regarding association with any not of their "stream." "Revival," my friend confesses, "is not even mentioned here." As a result, this church is perceived by multitudes as sectarian, and tragically, they don't even know it!

Other churches focus on revival to such a great extent that its true significance is lost. They want it so badly, or they misunderstand its true meaning, and, as a result, it becomes a formal event. Church marquees read: "Revival—This Week at 7 P.M." or "Revival Services With Evangelist Joe Dokes—Sunday 9 and 11 A.M."

My friend Dr. Michael L. Brown responds to this misunderstanding with this advice: "There are no shortcuts to revival. No formulas exist for a visitation from God. Only God can send the rain!" What churches that promote "revival" are really saying is: "We invite you to evangelistic meetings intended to provoke you to pray and witness for Christ."

Still others equate revival with anything that produces strange manifestations—people shrieking, shaking, barking like a dog or losing control of themselves. While God may move through any manifestation He desires (within the boundaries of Scripture), those same manifestations are no guarantee that God is sending revival fire. The manifestations may be from God, but they may also be fleshly responses to unusual activity of the Spirit. The manifestations may even be entirely provoked by the flesh and in need of godly oversight and correction to keep things on track.

But misunderstanding the true nature of revival defrauds countless numbers of Christians from experiencing what is both biblically and historically a genuine gift from almighty God.

Do You Have to Have Manifestations to Have Revival?

The subject of manifestations seems to be one of the greatest points of disagreement among Christians. Some well-meaning believers want nothing to do with revival; they know when the Holy Spirit comes in power, things can get a little messy. The leadership may lose a little control of the worship services, and people may begin exhibiting behavior you just don't see in normal, everyday society.

105

But consider how the Christians were perceived at Pentecost. Imagine walking down a dusty Jerusalem road and hearing a group of people singing and praying in an upstairs room of a nearby home. Suddenly they begin shouting in different languages, laughing and praising God with exuberance. You stop to listen to the commotion, but then everyone in the upstairs room comes rushing out to the street. And above each head is a mysterious flamelike glow.

Within no time you are surrounded by people speaking in every language you can imagine. You pick up bits and pieces of the different languages and conclude they're all basically talking about one person—Jesus. Actually, they're worshiping Jesus, the man who was nailed to a cross a month or so ago and who some claim rose from the dead.

The strange behavior of the people on the street eventually attracts a crowd. And what was the opinion of many regarding this strange behavior? "They have had too much wine" (Acts 2:13).

Was the Holy Spirit present at Pentecost? Of course. Was the behavior of the Christians a little strange? Absolutely, or they wouldn't have been accused of being drunk.

In light of the excesses that inevitably surface during every move of God, many people ask, "Can I have revival but skip the manifestations?"

While the focus of revival isn't upon manifestations (primarily, it is on your love relationship with Jesus), they are often an indicator that God is at work and that people have yielded themselves to the Holy Spirit in far greater ways.

How did the believers at Pentecost know that the Holy Spirit was being poured out? The wind was blowing furiously in the upper room, the people were praying in tongues and over every person's head was a tongue of fire. Some of the manifestations were under the people's control to some extent (praying in tongues), but others were not (the wind and fire).

Manifestations are God's way of penetrating the church's safe, secure world of control and dignity. Charles Spurgeon, the nineteenth-century "prince of preachers," used to pray for God to send "a season of glorious disorder." John Wesley prayed, "Lord, send us revival without excesses. But if excesses must accompany revival, then send us revival!"

What is the alternative? You can play it safe, avoiding any manifestations that could cause you to lose control. You can insist on a predictable, dignified, scripted worship service that includes a "nice" yet often unanointed sermon, and an obvious lack of the spontaneous and supernatural work of the Spirit.

The most important thing is to make your focus knowing Jesus and to allow the Holy Spirit to determine what manifestations will present themselves—under the authority of Scripture and godly leadership. John Wesley once said, "We will neither encourage nor suppress unusual manifestations." Sound advice!

MANIFESTATIONS *ARE* BIBLICAL 107

While many people desperately want a fresh move of the Spirit, some want the power without the manifestations. "I just want to be biblical" is their reasoning. But manifestations *are* biblical!

Here is a sample of different manifestations found in Scripture:

Falling

> ∞ Ezekiel is literally floored by the glory of God (Ezek. 1:28).
> ∞ In his vision of the preincarnate Christ, Daniel falls "into a deep sleep" (Dan. 10:9).
> ∞ Saul falls to the ground when confronted by the risen Christ (Acts 9:4).
> ∞ John falls at Jesus' feet "as though dead" (Rev. 1:17).

Shaking and "Drunkenness"

> ∞ Jeremiah experiences trembling and apparent drunkenness from God's presence (Jer. 23:9).
> ∞ Other Old Testament examples of trembling (Dan. 10:10; Ps. 99:1)

- ✆ The believers at Pentecost are accused of being drunk (Acts 2:13–16).
- ✆ The Holy Spirit's touch causes people and buildings to shake (Acts 4:31; 16:26).
- ✆ Paul compares being drunk on wine to being filled with the Spirit (Eph. 5:18).

Weeping

- ✆ People weep upon hearing God's Word (Neh. 8:9).
- ✆ A woman weeps in repentance at Jesus' feet (Luke 7:37–38).

108 Laughter and dancing

- ✆ "The One enthroned in heaven laughs" (Ps. 2:4).
- ✆ The anointing of the Holy Spirit upon the righteous is likened to the "oil of joy" (Ps. 45:7; Heb. 1:9).
- ✆ Forgiveness and a fresh touch from God is celebrated with rejoicing and dancing (Ps. 30:5, 11–12).
- ✆ Michal despises her husband, King David, for dancing and celebrating God's presence. As a result, she is barren the rest of her life (2 Sam. 6:16, 20–23).
- ✆ The Hebrew word for *rejoice* means "to spin like a top."

Not only were manifestations common in biblical moves of God, but they have been common in more recent historical moves of God, too. Notice that the following manifestations occurred before the restoration of tongues at the beginning of the twentieth century.

During George Whitefield's ministry in the mid-1700s, reports indicate that people were moved with uncontrollable sobbing, and some were "overcome with fainting." At the conclusion of one of Whitefield's sermon, those people who "fainted" were still "chained to the ground."

In 1769 John Wesley was confronted by an indignant Quaker who was disgusted by the manifestations he saw in Wesley's meetings. Suddenly, the man dropped to the ground. In obvious agony, he asked God to forgive him, then lifted his head and said to Wesley, "Now I know thou art a prophet of the Lord!"

The pioneers living on the American frontier of the early 1800s enjoyed attending camp meetings that usually lasted about four days at a time. Common manifestations included fainting, rolling, laughing, running, singing, dancing and jerking. One account reports as many as five hundred people "swept down in a moment as if a battery of a thousand guns had been opened upon them, and then immediately followed by shrieks and shouts that rent the very heavens."

The person writing the account then confessed, "I fled for the woods... and wished I had stayed at home!"

REVIVAL COMES AT A PRICE

Although revival brings spiritual refreshment to your life, there is a cost. R. T. Kendall asks pioneers in no uncertain terms what price they are willing to pay for revival: "Are you willing to bear the stigma of a new move of God in your generation? The paramount stigma of being today's and tomorrow's man or woman is probably that of being misunderstood."[3]

Luke 2:34 speaks of the invasion of God's purpose in the first century through the coming of His Son as "a sign that will be spoken against."

You mean it's not all blessing and glory?

Ask the pioneers of previous generations who "kept step with the Spirit" and paid for it with their lives!

Men like John Huss, Savonarola, John Wycliff and William Tyndale (all of whom I mentioned in chapter four) endured torture, ridicule or martyrdom in order to lead the church forward into new seasons in God's unfolding purposes.

Winkie Pratney, a close friend who also is a noted historian on revival, once commented, "We do not have men and women who are prepared to pay the same price to preach the same message and have the same power as those revivalists of the past!"

The men and women Winkie is describing may not exist as a majority. But you can take the mantle from a chosen few who have gone before you, laying down their lives so that others can experience a new dimension of the Spirit.

God is looking for a few good men and women who are willing lead the way into new realms of His glory. God may not call you to be a martyr, but it's possible you will face ridicule, misunderstanding and possibly even expulsion from people or churches who are either unwilling or unable to "keep in step with the Spirit" (Gal. 5:25). The rejection may even come from people you love and respect. But the cost is miniscule compared to the fruit that will inevitably result.

ARE *YOU* A SETTLER OR A PIONEER?

As this chapter draws to a close, please take to heart this challenge I am issuing to you: Be a pioneer by wholeheartedly yielding your life afresh to the One who calls you.

Settlers (in our culture) espouse an *American* form of Christianity that is characterized by comfort, convenience and compromise.

Pioneers live out *biblical* Christianity that is characterized by Spirit-led living, supernatural ministry, surrender to Jesus as Lord, service, sacrifice, stewardship and soul-winning.

Settlers are satisfied with slick, quick, predictable church services peppered with man-centered praise and worship and shallow "sermonettes." Settlers are attracted to worship in the form of performance and entertainment.

111

Pioneers yearn for fresh anointed food straight from the pantry of the "whole counsel" of God. They yearn for genuine New Testament community and God-centered worship that makes room for the Holy Spirit to lead, change direction or even interrupt church as He pleases. Pioneers are attracted to worship that draws them closer to Jesus.

Settlers worship the God of love and seek every blessing He has for them.

Pioneers worship the God of *holy* love and understand that God calls His people to a lifestyle of holiness and repentance while they enjoy His love and blessings.

Settlers are content to live with little, if any, supernatural or prophetic activity in their lives.

Pioneers hunger for supernatural prophetic ministry, and they yield themselves to the Holy Spirit so that He can perform signs and wonders through them.

Settlers give in to the ever-eroding moral standards of society (abortion, divorce, homosexuality and others). They may disagree with the "new" standards, but they do nothing about it.

Pioneers understand the seriousness of sin in their society, and they plead before the Father for His divine intervention. Rather than merely protesting ongoing sin, they seek to be part of the solution by living lives of "happy holiness" and inspiring others who see the obvious blessing, favor and anointing on their lives.

Settlers enjoy the comforts this world offers and seek lives of security, luxury and more stuff.

Pioneers realize life is more than security and stuff and refuse to make this world their home. They deny themselves daily, pick up their crosses and follow Jesus.

Considering these comparisons between a settler and a spiritual pioneer, please ask yourself, *Am I a settler or a pioneer?* If you find that you're a settler, this is a good time to pick up your stakes and launch out on God's wild frontier. Seek the restoration and refreshment that comes from God's renewing presence, and ask God to forgive you for being complacent.

Then join the ranks of the pioneers who are leading God's people into the vast unexplored regions of His glory and grace.

Eight

The Quest for Quality

When I first started out in ministry, God orchestrated a test I managed to pass—barely. This experience was a pivotal event in my life. I was a young Christian, and in my youthful exuberance, I was convinced that I was ready to take on the world for Jesus.

After relocating to the Washington, D.C. area from Cleveland, Ohio, I scanned the scene for areas of ministry that would launch me forward. Although my heart was in the right place—I sincerely wanted to serve God and His people—I was ignorant of the path that He desires for His people to take. While I was more focused on the *product*, God was more focused on the *process*.

I approached two leaders of a mushrooming ministry and shared with them that I was available and eager to launch a new ministry to young adults (they had none at the time). Wisely, they asked if we could arrange a time to get together for a meal and some conversation, which we did a few nights later.

"So, tell us of your thoughts regarding this youth ministry," asked one of the middle-aged leaders.

I leaned back in my chair and told them about my conversion two years before and my natural ability to connect with youth. "After all," I reasoned, "I was the student body president of Cleveland State University." I further explained that my earned degree in communications equipped me with the tools to speak in front of groups of people. "With my people skills and my ability to relate to youth, we should have a powerful youth ministry in no time," I concluded. (It's been said, "There is no such thing as a humble young man!")

Then I moved in to close the sale. "When would you like me to start?"

George and Bob glanced at each other in the bustling cafeteria. *I guess I really made an impression on them with my résumé and skills,* I thought. *I wonder if they'll offer to pay me something, too?*

"Larry," George said, as he gently smiled and removed his black-framed glasses. "We think you have lots of zeal and lots of good ideas. No doubt you're ready to hit the ground running. But for now we feel the best thing for you would be to prove yourself in obscurity . . . by taking down the folding chairs after our weekly meetings."

"Excuse me?!"

"Take down the chairs each week, Larry. There are about four hundred or so, and you can work with our existing crew."

"Huh? I mean . . . did I . . . was I not clear on what I'm gifted to do?"

Both men smiled as they intuitively realized the inner turmoil of my heart. Then Bob winked as he challenged me. "Prove yourself a faithful servant in little things, Larry, and Jesus will honor your labors and promote you at the right time."

Although I didn't realize it at the time, this was a defining moment in my life and ministry. While my emotions and flesh recoiled at the proposal, the power of the Holy Spirit and the grace of God enabled me to embrace His will for my life reluctantly.

GOD IS MORE CONCERNED ABOUT YOUR CHARACTER THAN YOUR SUCCESS

Christianity 101 is a course God requires every Christian to take. It's a class whose sole subject is character—faithfulness...humility...a teachable spirit...a servant's heart. All are prerequisites to promotion in the kingdom of God and the building blocks upon which a quality work is established. Faithful, humble service in secret precedes blessing and promotion in public. Faithfulness leads to fruitfulness. The principle is clear in the words of Jesus:

> Whoever can be trusted with very little can also be trusted with much, and whoever is dishonest with very little will also be dishonest with much.
>
> —LUKE 16:10

Secular companies innately understand this principle of promotion. Is it any coincidence that well-known TV personalities like Ted Koppel, Regis Philbin, Willard Scott and Disney chief Michael Eisner began their careers as pages—serving guests, leading tours and assisting audiences in the "little" things?

Kenneth Copeland began his ministry by serving Oral

115

Roberts as a pilot and by holding his coat during prayer times. A. W. Tozer served as editor for A. B. Simpson's Christian Missionary Alliance publication *Alliance Life* before becoming an influential preacher and author.

Thank God for His sustaining grace, which enabled me to respond correctly to some of my early ministry tests. If you could have seen me during those early years on those late Friday evenings after the weekly meeting for the ministry I had joined had ended, you would have chuckled. There I was—a young, upstart twenty-one-year-old *cum laude* BMOC (big man on campus)—employed in a "prestigious" job (working for the AFL-CIO across the street from the White House!). But on those Friday evenings I wasn't working my job. I was engaged in my first ministry assignment—stacking chairs, sweeping floors and picking up trash! I struggled, but I learned an invaluable lesson about servanthood, humility and faithfulness—one that I carry with me even to this day.

QUALITY TAKES TIME

When George and Bob assigned me to the clean-up crew, I thought they were crazy. *They need me working with youth more than they need me stacking chairs,* I thought. *Don't they realize that their ministry would grow faster if they had a dynamic youth ministry?*

I was focused on *quantity* while these men wisely valued *quality*. They wanted to test my true motivations as well as make sure I was mature enough to handle the responsibility. And they were willing to wait until God showed them it was time for "promoting" me into the youth ministry.

Pioneers who labor in God's kingdom build with quality in mind rather than quantity. They want to grow, to be sure, but they understand that quality eventually yields quantity. Slow, steady growth is preferable to explosive, uncontrolled growth. When growth is slow, character has time to develop. This is the pattern God establishes in Scripture.

> For you, O God, tested us; you refined us like silver. You brought us into prison and laid burdens on our backs. You let men ride over our heads; we went through fire and water, but you brought us to a place of abundance.
> —PSALM 66:10–12

117

> The path of the righteous is like the first gleam of dawn, shining ever brighter till the full light of day.
> —PROVERBS 4:18

While the New Testament church experienced a harvest that grew by exponential proportions, don't forget that God first tilled the soil through the ministries of John the Baptist and Jesus. John the Baptist prepared the way for Jesus, and Jesus prepared the way for His church. Despite the power and anointing Jesus demonstrated in His ministry, His followers numbered only one hundred twenty just before Pentecost. (He had appeared to over five hundred—where were the rest?) However, the quality preparation God provided at the beginning is what yielded the dynamic results at Pentecost and thereafter.

The adage "The best is yet to come" shouldn't be just a cute cliché—it is based on the Word of God. When you reflect on your life, you should be able to see how God used relational and circumstantial testing to mature you and move you ahead—even when you didn't want to move ahead!

No shortcuts exist on the journey to maturity. If you fail to respond in a Godlike manner to the obstacles God places in your way, you risk missing out on your destiny. King Saul, Samson and the rich, young ruler (in Matt. 19) are tragic examples of people who failed the character test. On the other hand, Ruth (the Moabite widow who became the great-grandmother of King David), Peter and Paul are examples of people from Scripture who persevered and realized God's plans for their lives.

118

Most people seek quick transformation. They want sudden deliverance from sinful habits and to be changed from sinner to saint in an instant. Unfortunately, many people who experience "sudden" transformation end up returning to the life they knew before Christ—quantity without quality.

How does God work maturity into your life? "Precept upon precept, line upon line" (Isa. 28:13, KJV). He's more interested in your roots running deep than in your branches growing broad. God is never in a hurry, and neither should you be.

People aren't dying and going to hell simply because you aren't fulfilling your vision for ministry. Take your time, and let God grow your roots deep, then launch you into areas of ministry in the context of the local church where you serve and are commended by your leaders.

Before launching into apostolic ministry, the apostle Paul spent nearly three years alone with God in the

Arabian desert (Gal. 1:17–18) and over a decade in formative, preparatory work. If Paul were living today, Christians would have pressured him immediately after his conversion to hit the preaching circuit and share his testimony of how God saved that high-powered lawyer and persecutor of Christians. If he had conformed to the pattern of many new Christian celebrities, within a short time he would have had his own program on Christian television.

Instead, he chose to grow deep before growing broad.

Posted over my desk are three maxims drawn from my friend and fellow laborer in the Lord, Charles Simpson. For over a decade they have reminded me to tread carefully:

119

> ∽ "God is not going to ask us how quickly we built, but how well we've built."

> ∽ "Failure is never fatal, and success is never final."

> ∽ "Consistency is a daily deposit in the bank of trust."

QUALITY REQUIRES THAT YOU WAIT ON GOD

Not only does quality take time, but it also requires God's timing.

In my three decades of ministry, I've had the privilege of authoring a number of books—with my last one released over fifteen years ago. Some people have asked me, "Why did you wait so long to write another book?" Believe me, the wait has not been easy, but it has been necessary.

Three factors restrained me from moving ahead: God's will, God's timing and God's word. Not only was

I willing to wait until He gave me the green light to write this book, but I was also intent on writing it according to His time line. Five years ago I couldn't write what I'm writing today because God still needed to work on some character issues in my life. He had certain lessons He wanted to work *in* me before He could communicate *through* me.

The fruit of that character development brought me to a new table of fresh manna. Until I was convinced that God had given me a word from His heart, I was willing to wait. You may have a general sense of where God is leading you, but you also need a word from God that gives you direction. And of course, you need to venture forward according to His timetable and in concert with local leaders in the context of the church where you are committed.

John Maxwell, the former pastor and respected leadership trainer, was asked why he waited two decades to write his book *The 21 Irrefutable Laws of Leadership.* "Twenty years ago I wouldn't have been able to teach them," he answered. "It has taken me my entire lifetime to learn and apply the laws of leadership to my life!"

If you are endowed with a pioneering spirit, then you likely get impatient waiting on God (as I do). But if you move ahead of His Spirit, you risk moving further and further away from His plans for your life. Moving ahead of God may reveal a prideful, unsubmissive heart. It may show that you believe you know better than God concerning the direction to take and when to go forward. Why do you think God ordained overseers in the local church?

Failing to wait on God's timing may also indicate that you think God needs your help—which He doesn't. God promised Abraham that he would have a son, but Abraham grew impatient because of his old age. The product of his impatience became a son, Ishmael, born of his slave woman, Hagar. Eventually the son of promise was born—Isaac—but the conflict that exists in the Middle East today between the Jews and Arabic peoples can be traced back to Abraham's disobedience four thousand years ago. (See Genesis 15–17.)

When you move ahead of God's will, God's timing and God's word, you will not experience God's favor. You'll encounter frustration and resistance. And in the end, you may not even accomplish your objective. But when these three characteristics line up, you'll sense God paving the way in front of you. He'll make your *121* crooked way straight and the rough places plain. Of course, obstacles will still cross your path, but you will sense God's presence and power giving you wisdom and strength to overcome them.

Best of all, the work that God accomplishes through you will last.

The admonition from Scripture is clear:

> By the grace God has given me, I laid the foundation as an expert builder, and someone else is building on it. *But each one should be careful how he builds.* For no one can lay any foundation other than the one already laid, which is Jesus Christ. If any man builds on this foundation using gold, silver, costly stones, wood, hay or straw, his work will be shown for what it is, because the Day will bring it to light. It will be revealed with fire, and the fire will test the *quality* of each man's work. If what he has built survives, he will receive his

reward. If it is burned up, he will suffer loss; he himself will be saved, but only as one escaping through the flames.

—1 Corinthians 3:10–15, emphasis added

Although we love to read reports of explosive numbers, we must realize that quick growth with enduring quality is a fantasy! And spiritual work *will* be tested. God's emphasis is on quality first with a view toward quantity (while avoiding the other error: "If it's small, it must be God").

Quality Requires Flexibility

122

The pursuit of quality also necessitates a large measure of flexibility. Often it is easy to become familiar and comfortable with the direction in which God is leading you. He may choose to change the direction, but you may want to continue moving ahead on the course you are on.

God's Word doesn't change, but times do. The message remains the same, but the methods are always evolving and adjusting. You may not like change, but to be a pioneer and not a settler, you must remain obedient in "following the cloud."

Over the past decade, Britain's Stoneleigh Bible Week Conference annually has drawn over twenty-five thousand people from over forty nations for worship, teaching and leadership training. Their CDs and tapes have encouraged and influenced people around the world, and their offerings received have brought millions of pounds into New Frontiers International, the host of the conference.

I've had the honor of ministering at these events, and, in my opinion, they are probably the most anointed convocations in the entire United Kingdom.

But recently, Terry Virgo, a longstanding friend and the apostolic leader of New Frontiers, informed me that he and his team were directed by the Holy Spirit to terminate their annual conference.

"The season is over. End the conferences in success. I have a new phase for this ministry," is what they heard the Spirit saying. And, true to their pioneering spirit, they remained flexible and discontinued the conference.

When you're a pioneer, you don't wait until attendance diminishes, finances struggle and the cloud obviously moves before concluding that maybe you should make a change. If God takes you from glory to glory, go with Him! You shouldn't have to prop up a lifeless meeting that has already served its purpose simply because God used it in times past. Besides, it's easier to give birth than raise the dead!

Often God's Spirit moves on to see if individuals, churches and ministries will depend completely upon Him and follow Him obediently into new frontiers.

God spoke to the Israelites just before they entered the Promised Land: "Be careful to follow every command I am giving you today, so that you may live and increase and may enter and possess the land that the LORD promised on oath to your forefathers" (Deut. 8:1). Possessing the Promised Land was not a one-time occurrence for Israel—it was a process that lasted hundreds of years and required countless battles.

The key to Israel's success was correlated to the extent to which they walked in obedience. In the same way, the key to your success (as God defines it) as a pioneer is correlated to the extent to which you obey the leading of the Spirit, even if it means discontinuing a ministry or activity that, at the moment, is fruitful and thriving.

QUALITY CAN COME FROM NEW CREATION

God's nature is to create. "In the beginning God created..." are the opening words in Scripture, and He hasn't stopped creating since. God told Isaiah, "See, I am doing a new thing!" (Isa. 43:19). In fact, variances of the word *new* appear 275 times in the Bible.

124   Starting something new, however, also means change, which can be painful. While writing this book, I was "hit" broadside by a major change. A series of events concerning the Brownsville Revival set into motion what I call an "unplanned pregnancy."

The Brownsville Revival School of Ministry in Pensacola, Florida (where I periodically teach) birthed another school—the F.I.R.E. School of Ministry (Fellowship for International Revival and Evangelism). Through what one of the leaders described as "the most difficult experience of my life," two schools emerged, both emphasizing revival fire, yet with different emphases. What lessons can be learned?

First, *some ministry ties are temporary, and some are life-long*. Paul and Timothy, as well as Billy Graham and his evangelistic team, are examples of fruitful ministry relationships that lasted a lifetime. On the other hand, Paul and Barnabas (Acts 15:36–41), the Brownsville School of Ministry and my own ministry experience (described earlier) are examples of painful departures that in the long run can bring new seasons of fruitfulness for His glory.

You may be laboring (at any level of ministry) alongside someone you love when suddenly you both discover that God is calling the two of you in different directions. Although your disagreement and departure may be painful, don't allow Satan to destroy your relationship with the other person or the good that God has already established through your partnership. Sometimes God intends good things to last as they are for just a season. Resist the temptation to decide who is more right in the departure—just trust that God is at work.

Second, *God often uses ministry separations and repositioning to reveal hearts.* This applies to both sides and to all parties involved. You can tell a lot more about people by the way they handle stress and their reasons for leaving than you can when everything is at peace.

125

Finally, *because God is sovereign, He can cause all things to work together for good* (Rom. 8:28, NAS). God is big enough to bless all parties involved—as long as they conduct themselves within the confines of His Word. Despite the pain, stress or turmoil surrounding the departure, He is well able to bring about His ultimate purpose.

Through the emergence of the two schools in Pensacola, God recruited more leaders into a deeper level of mentoring and teaching than if everything had stayed the same. God was saying, in effect, "I will continue to surprise you as I draft more experienced men and women into areas of mentoring the upcoming generation!"

As a pioneer, the temptation is to take the quickest, most direct route. But to God, the journey is as important as the

destination. Remember that the two hardest things in the Christian life are to love our enemies and to wait on God. Don't shortchange God or yourself by neglecting quality for the sake of quantity. Let God birth what He intends so the finished product brings the most glory to Him.

Nine

The Pursuit of Humility

I want to thank my Dad and Mom..." he began, smiling while trying to choke back the tears that were trickling down his face.

Che Ahn, my "son in the faith," was standing before the congregation that Sunday morning over twenty years ago, about to be ordained. While he was honoring his parents, I couldn't help feeling a little fatherly pride over the man I had spent years mentoring and with whom I shared a wonderful friendship.

"I'm grateful to my family members..." he continued. Just the day before, I had officiated at his wedding and although the two momentous dates left him a little disoriented that weekend, later that day he would quickly depart on his honeymoon.

"I also want to honor the men who have poured their lives into mine." He began listing the godly people— none nearly as close to him as me—while throwing in remnants of stories and describing their unique contribution to his life.

Sitting on the front row, my thoughts began to drift. *I*

wonder what he'll say when he gets to me? Sniffling a little and straightening my posture in my chair, I readied myself for the "big" moment as Che would single me out as the spiritual father who brought him to this hallowed place.

Che concluded naming the various people, and the applause subsided. Then he stepped back from the microphone and said quietly, "There is one more man I want to honor today." His eyes scanned the hundreds present as I gathered my thoughts.

"I thank God for his role in the plan of God for my life." I cleared my throat, preparing to share a few words.

"Lastly, I...I...want to honor...Charles Schmitt (a wonderful Bible teacher whose teaching impacted Che). Please stand." The crowd broke into applause while I sat there, stunned.

128

God pulled a fast one on me!

As I concluded my clapping and made my way alongside the other leaders to lay hands on him in prayer, I did my best to conceal my sadness in being forgotten. *How could he overlook me?* I thought. *After all the years, all the time, no one gave to him like I did.*

An hour later I drove home feeling physically spent and emotionally hurt. As the inevitable "Why?" circulated in my mind, I sensed the fingertip of God on my spirit. His still, small voice impressed upon me these words, "I let this happen on purpose, my son, to reveal what was in your heart."

My good Shepherd was going bottom line, and He was right. I was exposed. God made me aware of my carnal desires for recognition and honor by allowing me to be overlooked.

Subduing my flesh, I eventually repented and let God

know I was ashamed and truly sorry for my pride.

As I look back upon that event, I can't help but smile knowing that my immaturity was laid bare. God tested me to reveal what was in my heart and I must admit that I flunked. Royally.

Today Che Ahn remains my close friend as he leads the Harvest International Ministries (H.I.M.) network of churches and serves as director for the "The Call" International. We both laugh now at the oversight, but in a way I'm thankful for what happened. The lesson from God was loud and clear: He wants the people who serve Him to be men and women of humility.

GOD DOESN'T NEED ANY SUPERHEROES

The greatest danger lurking ahead of any pioneer is overconfidence. When you trust in your own abilities and seek recognition, you set yourself up for a fall. In order to be a pioneer of the spiritual sort, you must recognize how human you really are.

129

If you ever struggle with superhero tendencies, you are in good company. The apostle Paul struggled with pride, and as a result, God gave him a thorn in his flesh.

> To keep me from becoming conceited because of these surpassingly great revelations, there was given me a thorn in my flesh, a messenger of Satan, to torment me. Three times I pleaded with the Lord to take it away from me. But he said to me, "My grace is sufficient for you, for my power is made perfect in weakness."
>
> —2 CORINTHIANS 12:7–9

The power for you to minister as a pioneer comes not

from honed skills or extensive Bible knowledge (which are both important). The power comes from your acknowledgement of your *in*abilities and God *a*bilities. God's power is made perfect in weakness, and His grace is released in your life when you deflect all honor from you to Him.

Throughout Scripture God makes it clear that He will not share His glory with any other.

> I am the LORD; that is my name! I will not give my glory to another or my praise to idols.
> —ISAIAH 42:8

> Not to us, O LORD, not to us but to your name be the glory, because of your love and faithfulness.
> —PSALM 115:1

130

The classic Westminster Catechism explains it this way: "The chief end of man is to *glorify* God and enjoy Him forever." While you were created to enjoy God (the subject of chapters five and six), you were created to glorify Him, too. When you withhold the glory that is due God, you will find Him opposing you.

HUMILITY DOESN'T JUST HAPPEN

The apostle Peter wrote:

> All of you, clothe yourselves with humility toward one another, because, "God opposes the proud but gives grace to the humble." Humble yourselves, therefore, under God's mighty hand, that he may lift you up in due time. Cast all your anxiety on him because he cares for you.
> —1 PETER 5:5–7

God isn't neutral or passive about proud people. He opposes them. The Greek word for *oppose* in this passage, *antitasso,* is a military term that literally means "to range in battle against."[1] When you seek glory for yourself, when you take the credit for any success, you risk God battling against you. And the one person you don't want resisting you is almighty God!

On the other hand, God gives grace to the humble. Pride places God against you; humility places God on your side and unleashes the powers of heaven on your behalf.

Furthermore, Peter doesn't write, "You are clothed with humility." He writes, *"Clothe yourselves* with humility." Humility is something God won't do for you. It's not a fruit of the Spirit that is a result of the Spirit's work. Humility is an act of the will. That's why Peter writes further, "Humble yourselves, therefore, under God's mighty hand, that he may lift you up in due time."

God isn't opposed to exalting you. In fact, He wants to—but He must be the One doing the exalting! Exalt yourself, and God will humble you. But humble yourself, and God will exalt you—according to His time line.

Peter encourages you to cast all your anxiety on God because God cares for you. When you don't choose to be humble, it is easy to become uptight.

If I don't speak up for myself, who will speak up for me?

If I don't ask to sing that lead in church, I'll never get a chance.

If I don't broadcast my accomplishments, no one will know what I'm capable of doing, and I'll never have a chance to fulfill the dream God has placed in my heart.

You may have the noblest reasons for drawing

131

attention to yourself, but all of them are rooted in pride. Don't worry about being promoted. Be faithful in the little things, and God will make you a ruler over much (Matt. 25:23).

When you promote yourself, you circumvent God's time line and process for promotion. Perhaps He wants to work on a few more character issues before moving you on—issues that will make the difference between being an effective leader and an ineffective leader.

Self-promotion is the pursuit of quantity over quality, because it seeks quick results without having to prove itself first. It also places people in the position of trying to do God's work in the flesh, which requires much more effort than doing God's work by the power of the Spirit.

132

My dear friend Bob Weiner, one of this generation's outstanding apostolic leaders, once said that God pinpointed this verse from 1 Peter to him after he suffered a heart attack at age thirty-eight. He had tried to handle the stress of overseeing hundreds of churches in his own strength, and he paid for it with his health. Learning to humble himself, he discovered God does "give grace to the humble" as we "cast all our anxiety on Him." The greater the yielding, the greater the grace.

JOIN THE NAMELESS, FACELESS GENERATION

As God revives and restores His church, He is building the ranks of His troops with men and women of character. Through humility and quality they will march forward, unconcerned about drawing attention to themselves or building their own kingdoms.

Prophetic leader Paul Cain refers to this mass of people as a "nameless, faceless generation." They are consumed solely with the glory of God and care not what accolades or awards are bestowed upon them.

Dr. Michael Brown often exhorts the students and faculty at the F.I.R.E. School of Ministry by saying, "Don't forget why God brought us here. He is taking somebodies and turning them into nobodies for the glory of God!" The greatest aspiration you could ever have is to be nobody for God.

"God works best with nothing," Mother Teresa once said. And that is God's nature—working best with nothing. Genesis 1:1 begins with these famous words, "In the beginning God created the heavens and the earth." God created the world out of nothing and then called it *good* (Gen. 1:9). From the soil of the earth He then created Adam and called him *good* (v. 31).

When Jesus came to earth, He followed the same pattern. Read closely Paul's description of the incarnation of Jesus:

> Do nothing out of selfish ambition or vain conceit, but in humility consider others better than yourselves... Your attitude should be the same as that of Christ Jesus: Who, being in very nature God, did not consider equality with God something to be grasped, but made himself nothing, taking the very nature of a servant, being made in human likeness. And being found in appearance as a man, he humbled himself and became obedient to death—even death on a cross!
>
> Therefore God exalted him to the highest place and gave him the name that is above every name,

that at the name of Jesus every knee should bow, in heaven and on earth and under the earth, and every tongue confess that Jesus Christ is Lord, to the glory of God the Father.

—PHILIPPIANS 2:3, 5–11

How does Paul describe Jesus' actions when He came to earth to save people from their sins?

> ↪ He made Himself *nothing.*
> ↪ He took the form of a servant.
> ↪ He *humbled* Himself.
> ↪ He became obedient to death even on a cross.

And how did God the Father respond to Jesus' ultimate acts of humility?

134

> ↪ He exalted Jesus.
> ↪ He gave Jesus the name that is above all names.
> ↪ He promised that all people will eventually bow their knees to Jesus and confess that Jesus is Lord.

Most interesting of all is how Paul prefaces this weighty passage of Scripture.

Your attitude should be the same as that of Christ Jesus.

——PHILIPPIANS 2:5

Of course, you aren't God, and God will not someday have creation bow at your feet and declare that you are Lord. However, as you make yourself nothing, taking the form of a servant, humbling yourself and becoming obedient to death—even on a cross—God will exalt you. He will use you because you have become clay in the hands of the Master Potter.

Looking back over his eighty years of life, Billy

Graham wrote in his magnificent autobiography, *Just As I Am*, these words: "Most of all, if anything has been accomplished through my life, it has been solely God's doing, not mine, and He—not I—must get the credit."[2] Billy Graham was a twentieth-century pioneer for the gospel who models what the heart of a twenty-first-century pioneer should be like.

PRIDE BREEDS FEAR; HUMILITY BREEDS COURAGE

When the focus of your life is on self, you become fearful of man. You want to please people, and you seek their approval. But when the focus of your life is on God, you move forward with boldness, and you venture wherever God calls you to go.

135

As I have already mentioned, this is an area that God had to resolve in my life before releasing me into the next season of my ministry. For years I made little concessions and compromises to stay in the good graces of certain leaders and to avoid forfeiting privilege, promotion, provision or personal speaking opportunities.

By yielding to a fear of man I became enslaved to the pursuit of being recognized in ministry. My futile attempts to achieve approval and acceptance of certain people drove me even further away from the path God called me to follow.

This carnal, destructive pattern that had developed imperceptibly over many years had to be exposed and dismantled. What I needed was a death blow to my sinful nature. So God brought me back to the place of being nothing, where I could choose to take on the form of a servant, humble myself and, most painfully, become obedient to the death, nailing that self to the cross.

Finally, I could start over. But this time I was performing for an audience of One. The result was a new dimension of freedom from bondage to man that I had never known before. I enjoyed the new security that comes from pleasing the One who created me and already loves and accepts me. I was free to set out again on the trail of a pioneer.

> Am I now trying to win the approval of men, or of God? Or am I trying to please men? If I were still trying to please men, I would not be a servant of Christ.
>
> —GALATIANS 1:10

136 Seemingly overnight, I jumped from overseeing a network of churches to planting a small church in the basement of my modest home. Straying away from the "proven" methods of church planting to which I was accustomed, I chose to establish a church birthed in the fires of revival.

But I must admit that my new beginning was quite humbling, even humiliating. While attending a men's conference in Florida I was approached by a leader of a large church with attendance in excess of five thousand. He began our conversation by asking, "So how large is your church in Atlanta?" Ouch! Hearts are tested in moments like those! And what matters most to God is faithfulness before fruitfulness.

GET YOUR HEART CHECKED

Everyone should see a doctor at least once a year for a checkup. I think that same advice is good for

Christians. At least once a year we should visit the Great Physician for a thorough examination of our spiritual condition. Below are some penetrating questions that I hope will help you determine the state of your heart and your motivation to serve God.

1. Do I promote myself and my ministry, or do I leave promotion to God while I go about the work He brings to me?

Let another praise you, and not your own mouth; someone else, and not your own lips.
—PROVERBS 27:2

Do not exalt yourself in the king's presence, and do not claim a place among great men; it is better for him to say to you, "Come up here," than for him to humiliate you before a nobleman.
—PROVERBS 25:6–7

No one from the east or the west or from the desert can exalt a man.
—PSALM 75:6

2. Do I compete with others, or am I secure in God wherever He places me, content to glorify only Him while He providentially works out His plan for my life?

Should you then seek great things for yourself? Seek them not.
—JEREMIAH 45:5

Let us not become conceited, provoking and envying each other.
—GALATIANS 5:26

But godliness with contentment is great gain.
—1 TIMOTHY 6:6

137

3. Do my actions proceed from a pure heart intent on pleasing God or from selfish ambition that only pleases myself?

For where you have envy and selfish ambition, there you find disorder and every evil practice.

—JAMES 3:16

All a man's ways seem right to him, but the LORD weighs the heart.

—PROVERBS 21:2

Do nothing out of selfish ambition or vain conceit, but in humility consider others better than yourselves.

—PHILIPPIANS 2:3

Periodically it is wise to ask yourself, *Why am I doing what I'm doing? For whom am I doing this?*

A dear friend of mine has a glowing résumé. At different times in her life she has worked with political luminaries such as Senator John Glenn and Senator Barry Goldwater. At other times she has labored alongside Christian leaders like Kenneth Copeland and Marilyn Hickey.

But at the present time she is following the call of God on her life by caring for her eighty-four-year-old father. Yet Bessie is as aglow with the Spirit washing her father's feet as she is when she is in the limelight. The reason? Her identity comes from her heavenly Father, not from how well she performs or in being recognized. She is simply serving in a different type of ministry during this season of her life.

What would you do if you were in Bessie's shoes?

Don't be a somebody. Be a nobody through whom God builds His church and launches this generation into the final push that ushers in the return of Jesus Christ.

138

Ten

Authentic Christianity

Christians in the church today are witnessing what one leader described as "truth decay." Instead of adhering to God's Word, many evangelicals take a pragmatic "whatever works and will get people to come" approach. Pragmatism has its merits, but today it is undermining authentic Christianity and our call to biblical faithfulness.

In the process, the authority and sufficiency of Scripture has been sacrificed on the altar of church growth. And, as a result, compromise has crept in. Scores of Christians follow the latest trends instead of following the Holy Spirit.

Moses built the Old Testament tabernacle "according to the pattern"; as a result, the glory of God came. (See Exodus 40.) Paul instructs us to likewise do everything "according to the pattern" in building the New Testament tabernacle—the local church. (See Hebrews 8:5.) Yet look at what is going on:

> ∞ In the quest for more nickels and noses, many church leaders lean more toward political correctness, cultural relevance,

image promotion and the notion that size equals success in the eyes of God.

- Charismatic sideshows parade preachers of imbalanced material prosperity, self-promotion and embarrassing "flashy" lifestyles, which both the world and the younger generation see through as nonsense and hype.

- "McChurch" meetings are increasingly offered to lure more congregants with "in-and-out" express services featuring three upbeat songs, offering and a twenty-minute sermon- ette. One church in Florida advertises: "Express worship, 45 minutes, Guaranteed!" Some now meet on Friday so as not to interfere with weekend leisure pursuits.

- Pretentious and unnecessary labeling with prestigious titles is becoming widespread. Ministers' demands for limousine service, trinkets of worldly success, lavish homes, cars and use of public relations firms to gain visibility is gaining momentum. One recent full-page ad portrays the "new face of ministry" with such superlatives as "powerful," "seen in hundreds of millions of households," "modern ministry giant," "a ministry conglomerate like no other in the world."

- And what about the divorces, immorality, interfaith emphasis, strange mannerisms and gaudy surroundings?

Does it matter?

Isn't the task of the church to help people to be holy—not primarily happy? Aren't the true measures of the church still biblical faithfulness and glorifying God—not numbers or image?

By taking their cues from the surrounding culture rather than from Scripture, relevance in the church has

140

unraveled into relativism. The self-centered, individual-istic mind-set of Western civilization has created an entitlement mentality among God's people. Christians believe God wants them rich; they bristle at the thought of dying to themselves.

Biblical standards, which in years past were steadfast, have eroded. The divorce rate among Christians is the same as among non-Christians. Professing evangelical believers fail to see a conflict between their sexual orien-tation (i.e., homosexuality) or practice (i.e., premarital sex, adultery, pornography) and their faith. Abortion has become the family secret—frowned upon but never-theless utilized if "necessary."

Ungodly music, movies, television programs or publi-cations that contradict the principles of Scripture are not only digested by the congregation, but incorporated in the sermon as "relevant" examples. Men and women are feeding their flesh while starving their spirits. *141*

Well-intentioned leaders eager to experience growth have mistakenly led the church away from authentic Christianity. The attempt to reach more people with the gospel has resulted in slick, short, superficial, scripted services streamlined to get 'em in and out for more bodies, bucks and bigness. Whatever seems to guarantee success must be God, right? (Even if it pri-marily caters to man's selfishness.)

Certainly a place exists for evangelistic services that are brief and fast-paced. Yet, the attempt to be relevant and lure people into the church must not dilute the New Testament worship experience intended by God for the local church. You simply cannot rush true wor-ship any more than you can fast-forward character development.

A CALL FOR AUTHENTICITY

Despite the erosion of biblical standards, God is awakening His people to recover an authentic Christian witness, characterized by passion for the Lord and for His church to reach a lost and dying world. In God's book, being "culturally relevant" never substitutes for being spiritually sound. (See Appendix A: Characteristics of an Authentic New Testament Church.)

God *is* "seeker sensitive." He seeks the lost (Luke 19:10). He seeks worshipers (John 4:23). He seeks godly offspring (Mal. 2:15). But the people of God must not become so intent on being seeker sensitive to the lost that the saints suffer. Substituting a "seeker sensitive" service for the weekly believers' gathering in the quest for bigger numbers and a *nonoffensive* approach is out of sync with the Bible (unless, of course, the local church celebration service gathers at another time)!

In the new millennium, authentic Christianity will shift from a primary emphasis on church growth (quantity) to church health (quality).[1] The two are not mutually exclusive, but the goal the spiritual pioneer chooses will determine what the church becomes—compromised or authentically Christian. Today God is raising up a new breed of servant leaders committed to biblical accuracy and apostolic fathering of our generation.

THE SURROUNDING CULTURE: UNABLE TO DISCERN

Society today is not merely experiencing a temporary malfunction but a complete absence of moral foundations. The house isn't falling because the plumbing needs repair. Its foundation has been bombed, and now the walls are collapsing!

After centuries of influence on Western civilization, the Christian values that shaped people's lives have evaporated in a generation. During the last thirty years, the unthinkable has now become acceptable.

Until recently, most people agreed that abortion is murder, homosexuality is perversion and pornography is dehumanizing and exploitative of women. Not any more. Modern "enlightened" thinking says these are personal or political issues, not moral ones. The old definition of "tolerance"—respecting another person's views while maintaining one's convictions—now means that because supposedly no absolute standards of right and wrong exist, everyone must *accept* the other person's position as equally valid.

Lacking a foundation of absolutes, large segments of the population have lost the ability to discern between right and wrong. Rejecting truth, their thinking has become futile and the result is moral disorder. The apostle Paul described this downward spiral:

> The wrath of God is being revealed from heaven against all the godlessness and wickedness of men who suppress the truth by their wickedness... For although they knew God, they neither glorified him as God nor gave thanks to him, but their

143

thinking became futile and their foolish hearts were darkened. Although they claimed to be wise, they became fools...Therefore God gave them over in the sinful desires of their hearts to sexual impurity for the degrading of their bodies with one another...and received in themselves the due penalty for their perversion.

—ROMANS 1:18, 21–22, 24, 27

The moral chaos evident today is unprecedented in America's history. What will it take to jolt this nation into the awareness that this is the first morally neutral generation in its history? Schools and society teach youth that basic morality does not exist. But notice the blindness as "experts" fail or refuse to admit the connection between this foolishness and the staggering increases in crime, family breakdown and sexual havoc.

THE SEDUCED CHURCH: CONFUSED AND COMPROMISED

Unfortunately, the same moral confusion and compromise that is prevalent in society is also present in many churches and denominations. This should not come as a surprise. Paul forewarned Timothy:

The Spirit clearly says that in later times some will abandon the faith and follow deceiving spirits and things taught by demons.

—1 TIMOTHY 4:1

This Scripture doesn't say people won't be "religious," attend church services or even say they believe in Jesus and the Bible. To the contrary; it implies they will. In fact, in his second letter to Timothy, Paul warned that many people will have a form of godliness—while denying God's power to rule their lives (2 Tim. 3:5).

Because God's truth is rejected, confusion and compromise abound. Consider the unbelievable disputes over biblical authority, morality (including the ordination of gay clergy) and theology taking place among Protestant and evangelical churches. Bishops from some denominations even promote positions that run completely contrary to Scripture and historic church teaching over thousands of years. It's heresy!

The Stirred Christian: Angry, Dissatisfied, Committed

God said this would happen. He also said that with ever-deepening darkness would come ever-increasing light on His true church. Following a prophecy of the escalating depravity of society in Isaiah 59, God proclaims, "Arise, shine, for your light has come, and the glory of the LORD rises upon you" (Isa. 60:1).

145

Days of trouble are tailor-made for Christians. In a bankrupt system where people have exhausted the sin spectrum, God is preparing His bride!

Today the Holy Spirit is using the current demise of culture and the church to bring together authentic Christians of true biblical faith. He's "smoking out" the phonies who play religious games for their own benefit. God is setting the backdrop against which His glorious church can rise in purity and power.

Followers of Jesus Christ are rising up who are willing to, as the late Francis Schaeffer once said, "pay the price of responsibility regardless of what that price may be." They are no longer willing to sit idly by and

watch the world fall deeper and deeper into darkness.

God is fashioning men and women of quality and humility who will hasten the return of Jesus Christ and finally crush Satan under their feet. God's people are not going to end this age in defeat—but in victory as the most influential people on the face of the earth. (See Psalm 2.)

Not everyone will be converted, but society will be confronted. Not every one will like them, but they will be respected. Not every one will agree with them, but society will have to deal with them.

At this point, you may be asking, "What can I do to become a part of this?"

1. Feel what God is feeling: righteous anger.

Not long ago we sat down as a family to watch a "family" film about a young man who lost his leg to cancer and decided to run across Canada in a fund-raising venture. "His courage made an entire nation cheer" was the promotional billing. Sounds inspirational and wholesome, doesn't it?

Later that night I stood in the kitchen trying to understand why the producers peppered the dialogue with constant obscenities and featured the "hero" dropping his pants to expose his bare bottom on-camera to a group of journalists. I was grieved and angry. Has this ever happened to you as you abruptly exited a theater or turned off a supposedly "decent" video?

Is it OK for Christians to become legitimately angry? Absolutely. While we know it is wrong to be angry over things about which God isn't angry, do you realize that is also wrong *NOT* to be angry over things God is angry about?

God's anger is mentioned approximately five hundred times in the Bible. Romans 1:18, to which I referred earlier, says, "The *wrath* of God is being revealed from heaven against all the godlessness and wickedness of men who suppress the truth by their wickedness." Dr. James Orr once described this kind of anger as, "the zeal of God for the maintenance of His holiness and honor."

God can be legitimately angry, and so can His people. In Ephesians 4:26 Paul writes, "Be ye angry, and sin not" (KJV). The Greek word used here for *anger—orge—* means "passion, anger, wrath."[2] It is the same word that describes God's wrath in Romans. The verb tense of the word in this particular passage indicates that Paul is issuing a command. It is not an excuse for a bad temper but a biblical basis for expressing, with a right spirit, the holy anger of God.

147

Even as Jesus was angry when He drove out the forces corrupting the temple of God, so today must His people vigorously resist the forces attempting to desecrate the new temple of God—the church.

2. Following the Spirit's lead, embark on your own quest for authentic Christianity.

Once God gives you a vision for His church, you can never go back. You are willing to do whatever it takes to drink from the wells of authentic New Testament Christianity. I saw this visibly at a One Thing young adults conference in Kansas City where eight hundred out of two thousand people answered the call to give themselves to the planting of New Testament churches in the days ahead.

My parents were tremendous pioneers and an

inspiration to many. After a lifetime of religious activity, while in their mid-sixties they repented and yielded their lives to Jesus as Savior and Lord. Despite their advanced age, they later sold the home they had owned their entire lives in order to obey God and become part of a genuine New Testament church.

Now I'm not implying that you have to move in order to respond to the Spirit's leading, but following Jesus means complete obedience—not selective obedience—to go where He directs. The cost of following Jesus requires obedience in everything.

3. Recognize and act upon your need for a supportive environment to live your Christian convictions amidst a society hostile to them.

In a fragmented society where people are crying out for meaningful relationships, God intends for you to experience the stability of authentic Christian community in the context of a local church. "Let us not give up meeting together, as some are in the habit of doing, but let us encourage one another—and all the more as you see the Day approaching" (Heb. 10:25). As the day of Jesus' coming approaches, you will need a community of people who encourage you forward as a pioneer rather than console and comfort you to stay a settler.

Commit yourself to a local church family who are dedicated to building relationships rather than attending meetings and who want to live uncompromisingly for the Lord. Benjamin Franklin once said something to this effect: "If we don't all hang together, we shall all hang separately." Without a committed local church community devoted wholeheartedly to God and each other, you will not be able to succeed

against societal pressure or the compromised church.

As a corporate people, not merely as isolated individuals, we can pray intelligently, pursue Spirit-borne strategies and proceed together as a mighty, victorious army!

AN AUTHENTIC CHRISTIAN IS A DISCIPLE OF JESUS

"Don't take this little book unless you mean business about going all the way with Jesus! It will jolt you. It will revolutionize your thinking about what it really means to follow Jesus Christ."

I was sitting across the table from an older man of God whose eyes seemed to pierce through mine as he laid down his challenge. The date was 1971. The place: Alabama. I had been a Christian about two years.

149

The book he handed me was titled *True Discipleship* by William MacDonald.[3] I accepted the man's challenge to read it, and my life has never been the same. I still have my worn, faded copy of this booklet, rife with innumerable pen markings and marginal notes from an excited young zealot for Christ.

God used that booklet to open my eyes to the nature of true discipleship and authentic Christianity. The earmarks of a true disciple include:

1. Supreme love for Jesus (Luke 14:26)
2. Denial of self (Matt. 16:24)
3. Choosing the way of the cross (Luke 9:23)
4. Dedicating one's life to following Christ (Matt. 10:38)
5. Fervent love for one another (John 13:35)

6. **Unswerving devotion to Jesus' words (John 8:31)**
7. **Forsaking all to be Jesus' disciple (Luke 14:33)**

Without these, Jesus said, "You cannot be my disciple." A disciple is a Christian—there is no biblical basis for people who believe in "Jesus as Savior" but not in "Jesus as Lord." When you choose to be a follower, a disciple of Jesus, you accept the whole package: Jesus saves you from your sins, and you dedicate your life to serving Him.

> Not everyone who says to me, "Lord, Lord," will enter the kingdom of heaven, but only he who does the will of my Father who is in heaven. Many will say to me on that day, "Lord, Lord, did we not prophesy in your name, and in your name drive out demons and perform many miracles?" Then I will tell them plainly, "I never knew you. Away from me, you evildoers!"
>
> —MATTHEW 7:21–23

150

THE AUTHENTIC NEW TESTAMENT CHURCH IS THE DWELLING PLACE THAT HOSTS GOD'S PRESENCE

Scripture describes the church as a "dwelling in which God lives by his Spirit" (Eph. 2:22). When the people of God gather together as members of His body, they experience Jesus' manifest presence—because they are the *body* of Christ.

The New Testament Christians understood their membership in the universal church of Jesus Christ, but they also understood their responsibility as members of a local community of believers. Going to church can't save a person, but being a Christian, for the early church, was synonymous with inclusion in a local body. One simply could not be a Lone Ranger and a Christian at the same time.

Authentic Christianity was not a meeting people attended once a week. It was (and still is) a way of life. The believers in the Book of Acts *continually* **devoted themselves to teaching, fellowship, to the breaking of bread and prayer (Acts 2:42).**

To live an authentic Christian life, you need to be joined to brothers and sisters who share an all-consuming commitment to follow Jesus and be a living expression of His body.

The New Testament lists thirty different "one anothers" that describe the relationship between believers. (See Appendix B: The One Anothers of Scripture.) These "one anothers" are the relational "building blocks" of Christianity. Without them Christianity becomes nothing more than brittle formalism. By looking over the list at least two things will be clearly understood: 1) Christianity cannot be lived in isolation; and 2) Few of the one anothers can be fully exercised in a once-a-week public assembly alone.

151

The Bible's one anothers cannot be imposed or legislated from without. They must arise as evidence of the joyful working of the Spirit of God within. When God's love has been shed abroad in your heart (Rom. 5:5), that love spills over into other areas of your life. You unreservedly share your life and possessions with one another. This is not a novelty, but an extension of church life as Scripture records it in the Book of Acts.

In the late second century, the ancient church father

Tertullian wrote his *Apology*. In it, he described how Christians shared not merely a meeting, but a total way of life! His classic comment—"See how these Christians love each other"—still stands as a testimony to God's intention for this generation.

If the body of Christ is going to recover a visible testimony on the earth, one that once again turns "the world upside down" (Acts 17:6, KJV), they are going to have to get back to the basics by relating to one another as God originally intended in the context of a true New Testament church.

AUTHENTIC NEW TESTAMENT WORSHIP IS BASED ON THE TABERNACLE OF DAVID

God is restoring authentic worship! He is reviving Christians' hunger for His presence, and He is calling His people to pursue a biblical vision for worship. Worship borne from the heart of the Father cannot be hurried and packaged to fit neatly into a scripted, swift service engineered to offend no one and microwave God's people through some sort of feel-good religious experience.

In Acts 15:16, James, the brother of Jesus, quotes the prophet Amos saying, "After these things I will return, *and I will rebuild the tabernacle of David that has fallen,* and I will rebuild its ruins, and I will restore it" (NAS, emphasis added).[4] God was foretelling the day when He would restore worship according to the pattern of David's tabernacle.

Worship in David's day was dynamic, expressive and free! Before his reign, Israel worshiped according to the pattern established by God through Moses. But David instituted changes that ushered in a season of revival that Israel hasn't experienced since.

Compare the differences between worship in the tabernacle of Moses with worship in the tabernacle of David, which God is restoring today:

TABERNACLE OF	
MOSES	**DAVID**
Limited singing	Joyful singing unrestrained
No instrumental music	Instrumental accompaniment
No clapping	Clap offerings
No shouting	Shouts of praise
No dancing	Dancing before the Lord
No lifting hands	Lifting of hands
Worshiping God from afar	Drawing near to God in exuberant worship
Only the High Priest approaches the ark of His presence	Many carry the ark of His presence
Few psalms	Much psalm singing

153

Can you imagine living in David's day? After five hundred years of worshiping God from afar, David ushered the nation of Israel into the refreshing, reviving presence of God.

Here is an example of Davidic worship:

> When the LORD brought back the captives to Zion, we were like men who dreamed. Our mouths were filled with *laughter*, our tongues with *songs* of joy. Then it was said among the nations, "The LORD has done great things for them." The LORD has done great things for us, and we are *filled with joy*.
> —PSALM 126:1–3, EMPHASIS ADDED

In these last days prior to the return of Jesus to Planet Earth, He is renewing His people through praise and worship in the pattern of David's tabernacle—just as He promised in Acts 15:16.[5]

Looking over the comparison above, notice the resemblance between the tabernacle of Moses and some churches today. God is cleansing His church of passive, superficial "worship" and predictable "canned" praise services. He's exposing the entertainment mind-set (worship team as performers vs. worshipers). He is freeing people from empty rituals, lifeless liturgies and half-hearted, mechanical singing. Instead God wants to usher people into the joy of His presence. People are recovering praise and worship that is passionate about Jesus and characterized by creativity, anointing and purity. It is fresh, sincere and the overflow of a lifestyle of worship. And it's not restricted to a select few— everyone is hungry for God. Men and women are coming to church with expectant hearts because they anticipate touching the hem of Jesus' garment.

The early church in the Book of Acts—after years of decline—recovered the divine order of worship and enjoyed God's presence. The record of their pattern of worship is found in the New Testament letters. Their worship wasn't somber, sad and stoic. It was alive! Paul encouraged the believers to "sing and make music in your heart to the Lord" (Eph. 5:19).

Paul also exhorted them to "sing psalms, hymns and spiritual songs with gratitude in your hearts to God" (Col. 3:16). The psalms came directly from the book of psalms, and the hymns were prepared songs similar to the worship choruses sung today.[6] The phrase "spiritual songs" probably means spontaneous singing that is inspired by

154

the Spirit—what many would call "singing in the Spirit."

Envision the church gathered together singing Psalm 150:

> Praise the LORD. Praise God in his sanctuary; praise him in his mighty heavens. Praise him for his acts of power; praise him for his surpassing greatness. Praise him with the sounding of the trumpet, praise him with the harp and lyre, praise him with tambourine and dancing, praise him with the strings and flute, praise him with the clash of cymbals, praise him with resounding cymbals. Let everything that has breath praise the LORD. Praise the LORD.

Is it any wonder that the old, hard-line Jewish leaders thought the early Christians were out of their minds? Isn't this being repeated today?

THE NEW TESTAMENT CHURCH EMPOWERS APOSTOLIC MINISTRY

One other aspect of New Testament Christianity that God is restoring after nearly two thousand years is genuine apostolic ministry. For the body of Christ to come to maturity, she needs to embrace all of the God-ordained ministries outlined in Ephesians 4:11–13:

> It was he who gave some to be apostles, some to be prophets, some to be evangelists, and some to be pastors and teachers, to prepare God's people for works of service, so that the body of Christ may be built up until we all reach unity in the faith and in the knowledge of the Son of God and become mature, attaining to the whole measure of the fullness of Christ.

In order to experience New Testament results, the church must recapture the New Testament pattern—apostles, prophets, evangelists, pastors and teachers who equip (not entertain!) the saints for works of service so that the body might be built up. People with the fivefold gifts equip, while the simple, ordinary Christians carry out the work of the body.

The fivefold gift ministries are expressions of Jesus Himself. Jesus Christ—the great apostle, prophet, evangelist, pastor and teacher—has distributed to the church He so loves the ministry that He alone embodies.

> ❧ **The apostle** *governs.*
> ❧ **The prophet** *guides.*
> ❧ **The evangelist** *gathers.*
> ❧ **The pastor** *guards.*
> ❧ **The teacher** *grounds.*

156

Leading the way is the apostle. Scripture records, "In the church God has appointed first of all apostles, second prophets..." (1 Cor. 12:28). Apostles are not necessarily missionaries or influential authors or "higher ups" in an ecclesiastical system, or gifted administrators or even senior leaders in the body of Christ. Just because a man calls himself an apostle does not mean he is one. An apostle is more of a function than a title and centers around strategizing and fathering of those who are served.

Apostles operate as architects ("wise master builders"—see 1 Corinthians 3:10) for the ongoing building and extension of the church of Jesus Christ. Based on proven ministry in their local church, they establish translocal work in other churches. Chosen and sent with a commission by God, they use their God-given gifts to lay proper biblical foundations and then function as "building inspectors" for the developing churches. Local pastors, recognizing their limitations and needs, submit to this gift ministry. Empowering the apostle to function properly is his relationship of mutually shared trust with the churches and pastors he serves.

When working together, the fivefold ministry gifts comprise an apostolic team, with the apostle providing primary leadership. I heard one leader make this statement: "Apostolic ministry is not a flash of brilliant individualism, but of glorious teamwork." Based in local churches, they labor together in establishing new churches and oversee the rebuilding and ongoing development of existing churches.

157

The New Testament is replete with references to apostolic team ministry. In Acts 13 Saul (later referred to as Paul), Barnabas, John Mark and an entire company whose number is not recorded are sent out from the church in Antioch. Verse 13 reads, "Now *Paul and his company* set sail from Paphos, and came to Perga in Pamphylia" (RSV, emphasis added). Paul was the apostle who led his apostolic team.

The reemergence of genuine apostle and apostolic ministry today presents a historic challenge to the church—as well as an unprecedented opportunity. Due to their cessationist beliefs regarding the gifts of the Spirit (that certain spiritual gifts no longer exist), some churches and denominations deny the need or see any biblical basis for apostolic ministry in the church today.

Other churches acknowledge three of the five gifts, but they avoid the ministry of apostles and prophets because of past abuses (which is understandable yet not acceptable in light of Scripture). Yet other churches affirm the fivefold ministry gifts but admit they are uncomfortable actually putting them into practice.

May the church avoid "nullify[ing] the word of God for the sake of...tradition" (Matt. 15:6). Instead, they should be teachable servants, examining the Scriptures to discover the present reality, not just the past history, of God's gifts to His church.

Apostolic team ministry was God's strategy in the Book of Acts—and His strategy today. Settlers ignore or dismiss this as unimportant. Pioneers pray for it and pursue it.

158

AUTHENTIC CHRISTIANITY IS A LIFE TO BE SHARED

As a boy, going to church was the absolute low point of my week. For me, apart from trips to Doc Gaylore and examinations at school, I can't think of anything I disliked more than going to church. *Boring...irrelevant...a waste of time...* are words that best describe my early religious experience.

Upon my conversion at age twenty, I found a new dimension of living where a personal God became real, relevant and responsible for my very existence. I soon found myself amidst scores of converted people who identified with my early church experience and hungered with me for deeper spiritual reality.

In time I became involved in teaching a weekly

meeting. The attendance eventually grew to over two thousand young people. Dynamic praise and worship, anointed Bible teaching, expression of spiritual gifts, huge crowds and a regular stream of conversions meant we had "arrived" at God's ultimate.

Or so we thought.

I soon realized the fundamental difference between attracting an audience and building a church. I saw that God wanted us to bring people into a spiritual family, not merely into a weekly service. Upon close study of the history of the early church, I discovered that Christianity was a life to be shared, not just a meeting to attend. It was relational, not institutional. Our call was to "make disciples," not merely decisions.

My experience taught me that intensity of worship during a meeting is not an accurate barometer of the spiritual maturity of the people. God is not concerned with how high you jump during church but how straight you walk in your daily life—especially as it is lived out with fellow believers.

The believers in Acts 2 "continually devoted themselves to teaching, fellowship, to the breaking of bread and prayer." They were our role models. They gathered corporately "in the temple" and shared their lifestyle "from house to house." Why then shouldn't we?

Once we grasped God's vision of the New Testament lifestyle—Christians sharing their lives together—we set our sights on living that way. As a result, we were able to show others what it means to *live* as Christians, and our lifestyle validated the gospel that we proclaimed.

Our experience together evolved into birthing our first New Testament church in 1976. Then this New Testament model was duplicated over the next two and a half decades in cities around the world. Radical Christians who were committed to doing the will of God—no matter what the cost—joined us in the glorious recovery of genuine New Testament church life.

The Vision: Simple but Not Easy

God's eternal purpose for the world has always concerned people. His intention from the beginning has been to rescue hurting people from selfishness and sin and then fashion them into a redeemed community (a local church) in their cities, provoking onlookers to jealousy by the quality of life they enjoy. It's not complicated, but neither is it easy. As Jesus put it, it will cost you everything!

Demonstrating a heavenly lifestyle in the midst of a fallen world requires that Christians venture outside the confines of their safe, secure, settled lifestyles and be joined to others hungry for God and His true church in our day. The world is waiting. As someone once said, "The world will never see Jesus until they see Him in His church."

Impacting the world for the gospel hinges on the formation of a people who not only declare the alternative but demonstrate it. Nonbelievers are much more open to what Christians say when they respect them for who they are. For Christians to be Zion—the "joy of the whole earth" (Ps. 48:2)—means they must show unbelievers they are different, not because they attend a Sunday meeting and don't smoke dope, but because of the way they live and relate with each other. People in the world will be impressed not by creeds, meetings or buildings but by seeing changed

160

lives and once selfish, independent people formed into local churches that accurately portray God's purpose for His church.

Your challenge and mine is to represent a new social order that every human secretly desires to be part of—an alternative society where people genuinely share, help and care for one another. And there is a big difference between a traditional model of a church, having little impact, and a biblical model that truly is a threat to Satan's domain. (See Appendix C: A Comparison of Traditional and Biblical Models of a Local Church.) To a society where this is missing, only one word describes this: *radical*.

161

Eleven

Radical or Simply Biblical?

THE PIONEER'S PLEDGE OF ALLEGIANCE TO GOD AND HIS CHURCH

Recently I read an article in *The Atlanta Journal-Constitution* that reported on a national study funded by the Lilly Endowment. The article identified the three hundred "best" churches of the Protestant and Catholic faiths in the United States. Some of the three hundred were lauded for their innovative programs in empowering the poor. Others were singled out for the vibrancy of their congregations.

One congregation singled out in the report pioneered a new idea—ordaining practicing homosexuals as deacons and ministers! Their pastor was quoted as saying that he was proud of his flock's "openness to gays and lesbians." While I can't think of a better place for a homosexual to be than at church, the church should not be a place that validates a wayward, unscriptural lifestyle.

True, this church was pioneering a new idea, but it

was heading in the wrong direction.

By virtue of their penchant for walking ahead of the rest of society, pioneers can stray off the beaten path. What makes pioneers great can also be their undoing.

THE SEVEN PLEDGES OF A SPIRITUAL PIONEER

The goal of every pioneer is to make new discoveries that enhance daily living. They seek hidden treasure, but in their process of seeking, they don't want to lose their way.

In this chapter I will give you seven signposts—in the form of pledges—that will prevent you from straying so far off the beaten path that you can't find your way back. You don't want to be led astray, nor do you want to be responsible for leading others astray. So these pledges also bring a sense of safety to the heart of the wanderer.

Pledge #1: I pledge to be faithful to the gathering of God's people.

Commitment is hard to come by in society today. Offering the excuse "I want to keep my options open," many make no commitment to anything—even many in the church.

Some people are like spiritual vagabonds—they wander between a handful of churches, attending whatever church meets their fancy at the moment. Others are torn by the strengths of a few churches: "I don't know what to do. I like the worship at Central Christian Center, but I like the preaching at Faith Church, so I think I'll leave after worship at Central and then drive over to Faith in time to hear the sermon." Of course, that same person goes to a third church on Wednesday nights because of its vibrant, midweek teaching ministry.

While it isn't sinful to get periodic feedings from other churches and ministries, spiritual pioneers will flourish when they are connected and accountable to one local church. You can't be a part of a body when you refuse to be connected to it. Wandering from church to church is like getting a kidney transplant but then, just as it starts working properly, removing it a few months later and getting a new kidney. And then another.

Besides, if a tragedy were to take place in your family, who would be there to support and encourage you? If you never committed yourself to a local church, how could you be sure that the church would be there for you? And what about the people at church who need the unique gifts you have to offer?

You need the body (a local body), and the body needs you. By making a commitment to one body, both you and the body benefit.

164

Some people make a commitment to one body but then fail to attend on a consistent basis. Our fleshly desires are masterful at coming up with excuses: "I'm so tired..." "The weather is too cold..." "The streets are too slippery..." "I don't want to be legalistic..." "This sniffle could be the start of a cold..." "It's been a long week..." "Gotta catch up on my rest." The list of excuses is endless.

You can choose to act according to God's Word and not submit to your emotions. Of course there are some valid reasons for missing a Sunday service, but you must be ever vigilant to discern the enemy's lies that keep you from being consistent in your church attendance.

And let us consider how we may spur one another

on toward love and good deeds. Let us not give up meeting together, as some are in the habit of doing, but let us encourage one another—and all the more as you see the Day approaching.
—HEBREWS 10:24–25

Every day they continued to meet together in the temple courts. They broke bread in their homes and ate together with glad and sincere hearts.
—ACTS 2:46

The New Testament believers didn't believe in getting their church obligation out of the way at the beginning of the week. They met in the temple courts every day. They met as often as possible. They also believed that God had created them for a day of rest.

Remember the Sabbath day by keeping it holy. Six days you shall labor and do all your work, but the seventh day is a Sabbath to the LORD your God. On it you shall not do any work, neither you, nor your son or daughter, nor your manservant or maidservant, nor your animals, nor the alien within your gates. For in six days the LORD made the heavens and the earth, the sea, and all that is in them, but he rested on the seventh day. Therefore the LORD blessed the Sabbath day and made it holy.
—EXODUS 20:8–11

165

The word *holy* means "set apart"—set apart from ordinary days and dedicated reverently to God. Some people squeeze church between busy work schedules while others squeeze church between busy weekend leisure schedules. Regardless, God calls His people to set apart a day from every week to dedicate to Him.

Pledge #2: I pledge to give myself to biblical fellowship that transcends a weekly worship service.

If the believers from the New Testament church could see the kind of "fellowship" into which many Christians today enter, they would be astonished. "That isn't fellowship," they would say. "That's just going to a Sunday service."

As I have already explained, authentic Christianity isn't built on meetings, but on relationships. It is relational, not institutional. Rather than being designed for convenience, it requires commitment from its members.

The believers *"devoted* themselves to the apostles' teaching and to the fellowship, to the breaking of bread and to prayer" (Acts 2:42, emphasis added). The Greek word for *devote* means "to be busily engaged in."[1] Church isn't something you go to once a week. In fact, the phrase "going to church" is kind of a misnomer, because the church isn't the building—church is the people *in* the building.

In normative New Testament Christianity, a spiritual family of brothers and sisters in Christ cultivate a shared life in community. More than something people do at the same time (like going to Sunday school or a church picnic), true community is about building relationships. Acts 4:32 presents a clear picture of authentic community: "All the believers were one in heart and mind. No one claimed that any of his possessions was his own, but they shared everything they had."

Entering into genuine New Testament community involves a conversion (for me, as real as when I became a Christian) from being concerned primarily about your individual good to being primarily concerned

166

about the common good. You pass from surface relationships based primarily upon *your* convenience and a
desire to have *your* needs met to a relationship of
interdependence. You move from isolation into a
shared life and become concerned about the needs of
others as well as yours.

**Authentic community is the fulfillment of
Psalm 68:6: "God sets the solitary in families" (NKJV). No one in the kingdom of God
should be alone. The church was designed
by God to give every believer a place to
belong. On the other hand, there is no
place in the kingdom for the rugged indi-
vidualist. True community in the authentic
New Testament church is the antidote to
the selfishness and prosperity of
"American Christianity."**

Pledge #3: I pledge to apply the Word of God to every
area of my life.

167

Deception is not limited only to cults and false religions. Scripture teaches that you can be deceived
merely by hearing the Word of God and not doing anything about it.

> *Do* not merely listen to the word, and so deceive
> yourselves. *Do* what it says. Anyone who listens to
> the word but does not *do* what it says is like a man
> who looks at his face in a mirror and, after looking
> at himself, goes away and immediately forgets
> what he looks like. But the man who looks intently
> into the perfect law that gives freedom, and con-
> tinues to *do* this, not forgetting what he has heard,
> but *doing* it—he will be blessed in what he *does*.
> —JAMES 1:22–25, EMPHASIS ADDED

Notice how many times variants of the word *do* is mentioned in this passage. Think God is trying to emphasize a point?

Now it's your turn. If you like, circle the word *do* in its various forms in the following Scripture passages.

> Now that you know these things, you will be blessed if you do them.
>
> —JOHN 13:17

> Not everyone who says to me, "Lord, Lord," will enter the kingdom of heaven, but only he who does the will of my Father who is in heaven. Many will say to me on that day, "Lord, Lord, did we not prophesy in your name, and in your name drive out demons and perform many miracles?" Then I will tell them plainly, "I never knew you. Away from me, you evildoers!"
>
> Therefore everyone who hears these words of mine and puts them into practice is like a wise man who built his house on the rock. The rain came down, the streams rose, and the winds blew and beat against that house; yet it did not fall, because it had its foundation on the rock. But everyone who hears these words of mine and does not put them into practice is like a foolish man who built his house on sand. The rain came down, the streams rose, and the winds blew and beat against that house, and it fell with a great crash.
>
> —MATTHEW 7:21–27

Obviously, applying the Word of God to your life is very important to God. When the early church "devoted themselves to the apostles' teaching," they didn't just listen politely—they talked about it, they

168

meditated on it, and they lived it out. (See Acts 2:42.)

Do you want God to bless you and to be delighted in you as His own dear son or daughter? Then be a doer of His Word no matter how you feel. Biblical commitment in a local church translates into more than just sitting in a pew and evaluating the sermon. It means acting upon what the living God teaches you through His living Word!

> My son, pay attention to what I say; listen closely to my words. Do not let them out of your sight, keep them within your heart; for they are life to those who find them and health to a man's whole body.
>
> —PROVERBS 4:20–22

Pledge #4: I pledge to serve God by using my God-given gifts.

Charles Spurgeon, the renowned British preacher and author, once visited an elderly lady in a poorhouse. The tiny room was pitifully furnished. As Spurgeon spoke with the woman, he noticed a framed piece of paper hanging on the wall with some writing on it. In response to his curiosity, the lady said it reminded her of an aged, invalid man she had nursed many years before. To show his appreciation for her loving care, the man scribbled a short note of thanks and signed it. He died shortly thereafter.

After much persuasion, Spurgeon received permission to borrow the paper. His hopes were confirmed when he brought the document to a nearby bank. "We've been wondering to whom the old gentleman left his money!" the bank officers exclaimed. An exorbitant sum had

169

been sitting idle for years because the man had no heirs and the bank had no record of the man's will. Until now! The "thank you" note was actually the man's last will and testament. The poor woman had been living in abject poverty for years, completely unaware of her vast wealth.

Every Christian who doesn't use his or her spiritual gifts is like that woman. Churches are filled with people who are sitting atop hidden treasures that should be invested for God's glory. This shouldn't be! You can get started by examining a listing of spiritual gifts straight from the word of God.

A SURVEY OF SPIRITUAL GIFTS

People who are gifts

170

- ⊕ APOSTLE—A "wise master builder" sent out from a local church he has built in order to establish other local churches on a proper biblical foundation (Eph. 2:20; 4:11)

- ⊕ PROPHET—A foundational ministry laboring alongside the apostle in building local churches by bringing the necessary insight and revelation to motivate and direct God's people with a current word from God (Eph. 2:20; 4:11)

- ⊕ EVANGELIST—A proclaimer of the gospel of the kingdom with signs following and an equipper of believers to be effective in winning new converts to the faith (Eph. 4:11; Acts 8:5–7)

- ⊕ TEACHER—An instructor in the Word of God to establish the saints in sound doctrine as well as inspiring them to search out the precious truths contained in Scripture (Eph. 4:11; 1 Cor. 12:29)

> ❧ PASTOR—The local overseer, elder or shepherd who leads, equips and cares for the local flock of God's people (Eph. 4:11; 1 Pet. 5:1–3)

In addition to the Ephesians 4:11 gift ministries, which are gifts given to the church, there is also the ministry of the deacon (Acts 6:1; 1 Tim. 3:8–10). A deacon is recognized by the local church leadership to serve in any capacity that is needed for the ongoing life and health of a local church.

Besides people who are gifts to the church, there are also gifts imparted to believers by the Holy Spirit. In surveying these gifts, we should realize that each one of us will probably have a number of these spiritual gifts with at least one dominant gift.

Gifts given to people

> ❧ PROPHECY—To exhort, edify and comfort through Spirit-inspired "forthtelling" and, at times, "foretelling" the Word of the Lord (Rom. 12:6; 1 Cor. 12:10)

> ❧ TEACHING—To instruct others from the Word of God for their edification, exhortation and comfort under the anointing of the Holy Spirit (Rom. 12:7)

> ❧ EXHORTATION—The Spirit-led ability to admonish or urge someone to follow a course of action according to the will of God. In the New Testament, exhortation means an appeal, encouragement or admonition (Rom. 12:8).

> ❧ GIVING—The Spirit-born ability to make money and, in turn, give it liberally for the advancement of the kingdom of God (Rom. 12:8)

> ❧ LEADING—The ability to motivate, manage and move

people to fulfill God's purposes in their lives and in the church (Rom. 12:8)

∽ MERCY—The ability to naturally identify with, minister to and feel strong empathy for those who suffer misfortune or are experiencing hurt, setback and affliction in life (Rom. 12:8)

∽ WORD OF WISDOM—The quickening illumination or impartation of divine inspiration to see, understand and respond to life situations from God's perspective (1 Cor. 12:8)

∽ WORD OF KNOWLEDGE—The supernatural revelation of insight, facts and information apart from human reasoning (1 Cor. 12:8)

∽ FAITH—The Spirit-born ability to believe God for the impossible to accomplish specific tasks or overcome extraordinary circumstances (1 Cor. 12:9)

∽ HEALING—The supernatural ability to minister physical, mental, emotional and spiritual healing to those in need (1 Cor. 12:9)

∽ MIRACLES—The supernatural gifting to accomplish acts that are contrary to the physical laws of nature in the realm of the impossible (1 Cor. 12:28)

∽ DISCERNMENT—The divine ability to perceive the spiritual source in a situation and judge accurately between truth and error (1 Cor. 12:10)

∽ TONGUES—The supernatural linguistic ability to communicate in a language one does not understand, but is interpreted to magnify God and edify the church (1 Cor. 12:10; 14:5)

172

- INTERPRETATION OF TONGUES—The ability to super-naturally interpret the meaning of a message given by the gift of tongues (1 Cor. 12:30; 14:6)

- ADMINISTRATION—The Spirit-born ability to steer or direct affairs of the church (1 Cor. 12:28; Rom. 12:8)

- HELPS—The God-given ability to serve others by sup-porting them or relieving them of certain practical needs (1 Cor. 12:28)

- SERVING—The God-given motivation to serve in practical ways in order to meet a current need in a joyful manner (Rom. 12:7)

- SPEAKING—The Spirit-born desire and ability to communi-cate as a spokesman for God in an effective way (1 Pet. 4:11)

Additional Gifts, Abilities and Skills

- SINGING—The anointed ability to glorify God and inspire others through music and song (1 Chron. 15:16–27)

- TEACHER OF SONG—One who instructs and leads in the use of the ministry of singing unto the Lord (1 Chron. 15:22; 25:6)

- MUSICIAN—One who is able to play an instrument skill-fully unto the Lord and inspire others to play and sing for the glory of God (1 Chron. 15:16; 16:42; 2 Chron. 5:13)

- INTERCESSION—A God-given desire and ability to pray for the needs of others with special fervency and frequency (Isa. 59:16)

- CRAFTSMANSHIP—The God-given ability to design, build or repair items based on an inherent skill imparted by God (Exod. 35:30–33)

173

∞ SEAMSTRESS/EMBROIDERER—The God-given ability
to design and spin with the hands cloth items that reflect a
master craftsmanship skill ordained by God (Exod. 35:25,
35; Acts 9:39)

∞ WORSHIP LEADING—The anointed ability given by the
Holy Spirit to oversee and direct the musicians and singers
in praise and worship of a Holy God (Ps. 109; 139; 140)

In His sovereignty, our heavenly Father has designed
a place and function for everyone to serve in a local
church. One day we will give an account for what we've
done to discover, develop and deploy our gifts for the
glory of God. What the devil has hijacked from the
church is currently being reclaimed!

In Atlanta, Georgia, there is a pioneer named Eddie
Long who is a black pastor who teaches that the charismatic gifts of the Spirit are for today. His church is now
the fastest growing church in the South, with over fifteen thousand members and three hundred being
added every month.

He and other black leaders say their denomination's
attitude toward the Charismatic movement is equiva-
lent to "apartheid."

Long, pastor of the New Birth Missionary Baptist
Church in Decatur, Georgia, is at the forefront of a
nationwide effort to gain acceptance for the
Charismatic movement within Baptist churches. Some
joke that they have become "Bapticostals"!

Eddie says the charismatic dimension is spreading
"like wildfire." As people serve in line with their gifts and
in the power of the Spirit, God will shake the traditions,
and normal New Testament Christianity will be restored!

As the resurgence of New Testament

174

Christianity captivates churches around the world, leaders are understanding God's original intention for His church as outlined in Ephesians 4:11–16. *It is not the responsibility of the leaders to put on a service for the saints; it is the responsibility of the leaders to equip the saints for service!*

Here are six suggestions for getting started in discovering, developing and deploying your spiritual gifts for God's glory and the growth of His church.

Consider—God has invested into your life certain gifts and abilities. Like the poor lady whose fortune Charles Spurgeon uncovered, far too many Christians waste their lives sitting in needless spiritual poverty. Begin by prayerfully studying the passages of Scripture that explain spiritual gifts: Romans 12:3–8; 1 Corinthians 12–14; Ephesians 4:11–13; 1 Peter 4:10–11.[2] Trust the Holy Spirit to guide your inquiry.

Covet—Years ago our son Justin was diagnosed with an eye condition that caused one of his eyes to cross. Doris and I earnestly sought God for his healing—praying every day as well as fasting on occasion. We brought him to one of the world's finest ophthalmologists who told us, "Your son will *always* need glasses." But God reminded me to "imitate those who through faith and patience inherit what has been promised" (Heb. 6:12). Rather than expect Justin's eyesight to deteriorate or merely stabilize, we prayed daily for his eyes to become stronger, believing that "with God all things are possible" (Matt. 19:26).

One day I received a phone call from then ten-year-old Justin. "Dad! Guess what? We're at Dr. Parks' office, and he just told me I won't have to wear glasses anymore!"

175

When my wife came on the line she explained the doctor's report: Justin was healed! We both tearfully praised God for the healing He had accomplished after seven long years!

My reason for mentioning this story is not to promote any simplistic formula for healing. God's faithfulness healed my son. But perseverance is required in order to receive all that God has in store for you.

This same sense of urgency and passion is implied in Paul's command to "eagerly desire spiritual gifts" (1 Cor. 14:1). The Greek expression rendered as "eagerly desire" could also be translated "covet earnestly." Though your neighbor's house and Mercedes Benz are off limits (Exod. 20:17), you're commanded to be white-hot in your pursuit of God and in coveting his generous gifts.

No shortcuts exist to discovering, developing and deploying your spiritual gifts. Minimum dedication will never lead to maximum blessing! The passionate—not the passive—discover that "he rewards those who earnestly seek him" (Heb. 11:6).

Contribute—Be careful not to focus so intently on pursuing *your* unique calling that you forget the main goal of the Christian life—serving God and others. The current culture of consumerism preaches the gospel of "looking out for number one." But Jesus declared, "It is more blessed to give than to receive" (Acts 20:35).

Rather than pursuing spiritual gifts with a view toward personal prominence, God is most pleased when His people's greatest desire is His honor and when their highest aspiration is to see the church revived, no matter how small or invisible their contribution may seem.

Consecrate—In Romans 12, Paul calls Christians to a life of consecration, a life willingly placed at God's disposal for whatever act of service He desires. Only this voluntary submission to God and His purposes will make your service effective.

After calling people to offer their bodies as living sacrifices transformed by the renewing of their minds, he warns them to view themselves with sober judgment. Then, in the context of consecrating themselves to God, he writes, "Just as each of us has one body with many members, and these members do not all have the same function, so in Christ we who are many form one body, and each member belongs to all the others. We have different gifts, according to the grace given us" (Rom. 12:4–6).

You are most effective using your gifts when you have offered yourself unreservedly to God. You did not choose Him; He chose you. You did not choose your spiritual gifts; God chose them for you. And you will experience the full extent of God's plans for your life when you dedicate them to His purposes.

Cultivate—The old cliché "Use it or lose it" has simple but profound significance when applied to spiritual gifts. Faithfully using a gift increases its effectiveness; failure to develop a gift curtails its effectiveness. Paul advised Timothy, "Do not neglect the spiritual gift within you" (1 Tim. 4:14, NAS).

One of the most effective communicators of Scripture I've heard over the years is Bob Mumford. He began his ministry by teaching learning disabled adults. Bob had to learn to be simple, clear and illustrative in order to

177

connect with his audience. Now, years later, Christians around the world benefit from a man who has finely tuned his gift.

Consult—Ask yourself the following questions:

1. **In what area of ministry do I sense the greatest anointing, fulfillment and results?**

2. **What do I sense is an area of critical need that stirs me, motivates me and compels me to action?**

3. **If I had all the resources, people, time and money I needed at my disposal, were in the center of God's will and knew I could not fail, what would I pursue to bring glory to God?**

When a person is drawn toward a certain area of service, it often reveals the presence of a corresponding spiritual gift. After all, God equips His people to accomplish His purposes. He doesn't take schizophrenic pleasure in choosing a tone-deaf worship leader or calling left-brained statisticians to head up the drama team.

178

How do people discover their singing talent? They find that they naturally gravitate toward singing. Or if a person has an inward desire to teach the Scriptures, he probably enjoys studying the Word of God and encouraging others with his insights. But oftentimes it requires other people in the body to identify what you're good at.

Gifts in the body will always be affirmed by others in the body—which is why it is important to cooperate with people in your church in discovering where your gifts lie. Because it comes so naturally, you may not even realize you're gifted at something until someone points it out to you.

Dr. Peter Wagner, formerly of Fuller Seminary, advises

people to develop their giftings in concert with existing church leadership. I wholeheartedly agree. The opportunity to receive training, encouragement and adjustment is a fundamental tenet of New Testament Christianity and one of the reasons placement in a local church is so critical.

Besides pastoral leadership, it's helpful to consult other gifted people who function proficiently in your area of gifting. Observe them, ask how they discovered their gifts and inquire about resource material they would recommend.

Don't squander your life in the poorhouse while you sit on your spiritual inheritance. Discover the exhilarating life of a pioneer by selflessly, systematically and skillfully using your spiritual gifts.[3]

Pledge #5: I pledge to be faithful with my financial support.

God instituted a plan to bless His people and to provide for the work of the ministry. It applies to every Christian as a *privilege* and a *responsibility*. It's a "get to," not so much a "have to." The plan is outlined in Malachi 3, and calls us to bring our "tithes and offerings into the storehouse" (the place of our spiritual feeding and oversight—our local church). Then we believe God to "open the floodgates of heaven and pour out so much blessing that you will not have enough room for it" (Mal. 3:10).

God calls us in the New Testament not only to honor His eternal plan, but, as those under grace, to exceed the minimum starting point to enter new levels of generosity and blessing. Yet few things will sidetrack a pioneer quicker than finances. The quest for money and stuff can easily stifle the dream God has placed in your heart—especially living in today's materialistic culture.

Some Bible teachers will tell you that God wants you to be rich. Others will tell you that if you really want to be spiritual, you need to be poor. So which one is correct?

Here are six biblical principles to help you keep your spiritual bearings straight while giving your tithes and offerings and to help you avoid imbalances amidst the prosperity/poverty debate:

> **Principle #1: Believe that your generous heavenly Father wants you to prosper.** Paul wrote that Jesus Christ became poor so that you "through his poverty might become rich" (2 Cor. 8:9). Does that mean God wants you prosperous? If your definition of "rich" suggests an ever-expanding paycheck, bigger homes, more expensive cars and fancier vacations, then your definition isn't from Scripture. Biblical prosperity centers first on giving (with a right motive) that leads to receiving in order to continue the cycle of blessing.
>
> > And God is able to make all grace abound to you, so that in all things at all times, having all that you need, you will abound in every good work…You will be made rich in every way so that you can be generous on every occasion, and through us your generosity will result in thanksgiving to God.
> > —2 Corinthians 9:8, 11
>
> **God wants you to prosper so that you can**

180

prosper others! Simply put, *prosperity* is "having enough for your needs with enough left over for others." You are a conduit of God's blessing to the world. You are blessed to be a blessing (Gen. 12:3).

Scripture, however, emphasizes God's care for your prosperity in *all* **areas of life—not just in your finances. John wrote, "I pray that in all respects you may prosper and be in good health, just as your soul prospers" (3 John 2, NAS).**

God is the creator of all wealth. He plans to share His prosperity with you for His glory and the expansion of His kingdom. He wants to bless you materially so you can enjoy life, share with others in need and carry out His will to make the nations His inheritance (Ps. 2:8).

Principle #2: Recognize God as your Source. "But remember the LORD your God, for it is he who gives you the ability to produce wealth" (Deut. 8:18). This passage is a reminder that banks, the government, your employer or even your abilities are not the source of your happiness and prosperity. They are instruments that can fail you, but God is your ultimate provider, and He will never fail you.

Principle #3: Discipline your spending habits. Americans have an amazing capacity for confusing their wants with their needs. As a result, they live beyond their means and use credit to buy things that they "can't live without." Soon the boomerang comes back, and they're faced with the pressure of bills and feelings of guilt because they can't give more to God. This lifestyle has created a new and strange phenomenon—the middle-class poor.

Often the problem isn't poverty—it's *discipline*. Every Christian should live by a realistic budget that includes monthly expenses, tithes and offerings and saving for future anticipated needs.

Principle #4: Sow to reap a harvest. "Give, and it will be given to you" (Luke 6:38). The law of sowing and reaping is found in both Scripture and nature. You receive (reap) as a result of giving (sowing), and you can expect to receive in abundance when giving according to His will! "Remember this: Whoever sows sparingly will also reap sparingly, and whoever sows generously will also reap generously" (2 Cor. 9:6).

A number of years ago my wife and I had an opportunity to invest the largest sum of money we've ever given into the cause of Christ and His church. After prayer, we took a large amount of the anticipated profit from the upcoming sale of our home and sowed it into a church-based ministry. Giving according to our ability—and then beyond our ability (2 Cor. 8:3), we dared to believe God for a rich return. Exactly three months later when our home was finally sold, we accrued a profit two and a half times our gift—far beyond what any real estate agent said we could possibly get for it! Selling the home ourselves without the benefit of a real estate agent enabled us to step into a realm that defied natural wisdom. Unbelieving onlookers called it "uncanny." We simply looked at it as God's miracle provision for two people daring to take God at his Word.

Principle #5: Give out of sacrifice, not only surplus. Giving out of surplus requires little faith. God wants His people to give sacrificially, like the widow He commended in Mark 12:44. When we do, we can watch Him supply our needs supernaturally.

Paul encouraged the Corinthians to follow the example of the Macedonians, who gave sacrificially, willingly and eagerly (2 Cor. 8:1–7). He also promised them a generous return for their obedience (2 Cor. 9:6–11).

183

Principle #6: Give in faith, and then persevere in faith.

> Let us not become weary in doing good, for at the proper time we will reap a harvest if we do not give up.
>
> —GALATIANS 6:9

After giving your tithe, offering or special pledge in a meeting charged with faith, it is easy to go home and find your faith level near empty when you face the normal financial challenges of life. It is important to remember that Satan is the thief (John 10:10), and he will do whatever he can to undermine your decision. Faith doesn't grow primarily in your faith-filled meeting, but in the battlefield of daily life!

When investing resources into God's kingdom, keep alert for the creative ways that God supplies. It's either coming toward you or going by you, often in unspectacular ways—a sale; an IRS refund. That's the adventure of serving the living God!

Does God want you to be rich and enjoy your covenant inheritance? Most assuredly yes! But He wants you to be a *channel* **rather than a reservoir so He can accomplish His purposes in the earth.**[4]

Pledge # 6: I pledge to honor pastoral oversight in my life. God never intended for the church to be a Christian free-for-all. A body whose different parts act on their own is not a sign of health, but of sickness. And although Christ is the head of the body, He also appoints leaders—authorities—who act as God's delegated overseers in the church.

Scripture is clear that every Christian needs to be properly related and submitted to the authorities God has placed over them. "Obey your leaders and submit to their authority. They keep watch over you as men who must give an account. Obey them so that their work will be a joy, not a burden, for that would be of no advantage to you" (Heb. 13:17).

In a society that is growing increasingly rebellious, submitting to authority requires humility. You may not always agree with the leaders God has placed over you, but that is not a license to run. Pray for your leaders, share your concerns with your leaders, submit to your

184

leaders (as long as they aren't abusive or heretical), and trust that they must answer to God for their teaching, decisions and actions.

It's easy to second-guess decisions that are made when the buck doesn't stop with you. Esteem your leaders, allowing them to equip you for your sphere of ministry, and you will grow in character, gifting and God's blessing. Dishonor the leaders that God has placed in your life, and you will miss growing in maturity and experiencing God's best for your life.

> Now we ask you, brothers, to respect those who work hard among you, who are over you in the Lord and who admonish you. Hold them in the highest regard in love because of their work. Live in peace with each other.
>
> —1 Thessalonians 5:12–13

Pledge #7: I pledge my loyalty to the body and to resolve all conflicts biblically. The church is a company of imperfect people learning to live a new life in a new way. Because it is inhabited by imperfect people, sin, offense, hurt and conflict are inevitable. What is most important to God is that we remain committed to each other in the face of conflict and deal with one another charitably and redemptively. At all times we must guard against bitterness, anger, slander, gossip and unforgiveness.

185

Nothing will hinder God's presence in your midst like internal conflict. Conflict literally stops the flow of the Holy Spirit. That is why God goes to great lengths to give His people instruction on working through conflict. Paul urged believers to "make every effort to keep the unity of the Spirit through the bond of peace" (Eph.

4:3). Peace doesn't just happen—it is the product of intentional effort and a commitment to one another.[5]

If every spiritual pioneer—and every believer—lived by the principles Jesus outlined in Matthew 18:15 regarding resolving conflict and reconciliation, the church would become a place that would cause the world to take notice. The power and anointing accompanies the purity and unity.

Take some time to review carefully these seven pledges. Which of the seven pledges have you made a part of your commitment as a Christian? Which do you need to strengthen in your own life? How will you develop these principles in your life? Now prayerfully consider how you can work as a body of believers in your local church to be sure these pledges are a part of your church life. What can you do to help your body practice these principles?

Living out these pledges will glorify God and enable us to experience more of His presence and express more of His power to a watching world.

Let's ask ourselves: "Are these pledges derived from Scripture *radical* or simply *biblical?*"

What I have described is not abnormal—it is normal Christianity. The church has been subnormal for so long that as it becomes normal, it will probably be seen as abnormal. It's time for spiritual pioneers to lead the way—with reckless abandon!

Twelve

The Call for a Righteous Revolution

ADULTS AND YOUTH TOGETHER IN A MULTIGENERATIONAL MOVEMENT

Maly, Maly!" the crowd chanted that Christmas Eve night in 1989. Vaclav Maly, a defrocked Catholic priest, had become the focal point of Czechoslovakia's "Velvet Revolution."

Since 1981, the Communist government had assigned Maly to clean toilets in the Prague subway system for preaching the gospel. But eight years later, as the Communist regime began crumbling, the people turned to the man who introduced them to freedom.

187

The incessant calls of "Maly, Maly!" by eight hundred thousand people crowded onto the streets beckoned this spiritual pioneer from the belly of Prague's subway system. As he emerged, he led the throng into the Old Town Square and then conducted an impromptu church service, offering forgiveness to his former Communist captors. By the hundreds, people answered Maly's call to come forward and repent for their past and to begin a new future.

And that is how Czechoslovakia's revolution took place. No bloodshed. No violence.

Vaclav Havel, the formerly imprisoned poet who became president, met with Maly and offered him the kingdom. "Father Maly, you can be anything you want in this government, from prime minister on down."

"Oh no!" Maly replied. "I just want to preach the gospel. I just want to tell people about Jesus." Then he returned to his church.

A RIGHTEOUS REVOLUTION IS ALREADY UNDERWAY

The smell of a righteous revolution is in the air—a revolution led by pioneers in the faith like Vaclav Maly. Governments may not be overthrown, but hearts will be transformed as men and women answer God's call to live and proclaim authentic Christianity.

Authentic Christianity has been and will always be a subversive movement. Governments that oppress and deprive people of basic freedoms will always perceive Christianity as a threat, because the secret to this revolution is the transformation of human hearts. Other cults and religions may gain converts by coercion, manipulation or even at the point of a loaded gun, but Christianity thrives when people experience the freedom of *choosing* to follow Jesus.

Spiritual pioneers follow a revolutionary leader; they share a revolutionary message; they live a revolutionary lifestyle. *Christianity is revolutionary. In this season of revival and restoration, men and women of God are recapturing what began two thousand years ago.*

188

The battle that has been raging for centuries is not a contest between Christianity and Islam, Christianity and Hinduism or Christianity and New Age religion. Increasingly, society is witnessing the contrast between the two conflicting kingdoms—the kingdom of this world and the kingdom of God. Consider the contrast:

THE TWO CONFLICTING KINGDOMS

THE KINGDOM OF THIS WORLD	THE KINGDOM OF GOD
Satan—"The god of this world" (2 Cor. 4:4, NAS)	Jesus—"Jesus Christ is Lord" (Phil. 2:11)
WORLDLY PRINCIPLES	**KINGDOM PRINCIPLES**
1. Seeing is believing.	1. Believing is seeing (John 20:29).
2. Attain wisdom.	2. Become a fool (1 Cor. 3:18).
3. Save your life.	3. Lose your life (Matt. 16:25).
4. Be first.	4. Be last (Mark 9:35).
5. Achieve greatness.	5. Become least (Luke 9:48).
6. Be a leader.	6. Become a servant (Mark 10:43).
7. Exalt yourself.	7. Humble yourself (Luke 14:11).
8. Take the front seat.	8. Take a back seat (Luke 14:10).
9. Look out for your own interests.	9. Look out for the interests of others (Phil. 2:4).
10. Receive much.	10. Give much (Luke 6:38).
11. Make your good deeds known.	11. Keep your good deeds secret (Matt. 6:3–4).
12. Loving is a conditional feeling.	12. Love is a lasting, unconditional commitment (1 Cor. 13).
13. Love grows old.	13. Love never fails (1 Cor. 13:8).
14. Hate your enemies.	14. Love your enemies (Matt. 5:44).
15. Retaliate.	15. Forgive (Col. 3:13).
16. Judge others.	16. Judge not (Matt. 7:1).

189

17.	Cover your mistakes.	17.	Confess your mistakes (James 5:16, KJV).
18.	Emphasize human might and human power.	18.	It is "not by might, nor by power, but by my spirit" (Zech. 4:6).
19.	Set up a guaranteed annual wage.	19.	"Give us today our daily bread" (Matt. 6:11).
20.	Eat, drink and be merry, for tomorrow we die.	20.	"Man shall not live on bread alone" (Matt. 4:4).
21.	Drown your sorrows.	21.	"Be filled with the Spirit" (Eph. 5:18).
22.	It is impossible.	22.	"Everything is possible for him who believes" (Mark 9:23).
23.	Check your stars.	23.	"Study the scriptures" (John 5:39).
24.	Scripture was written by man.	24.	All Scripture is given by inspiration of God (2 Tim. 3:16).
25.	The Bible is outdated.	25.	"Heaven and earth will pass away, but my words will never pass away" (Matt. 24:35).
26.	Jesus was a good man.	26.	Jesus is Lord! (Phil. 2:11).
27.	Jesus is dead.	27.	"Jesus Christ is the same yesterday and today and forever!" (Heb. 13:8).
28.	Jesus is not coming again.	28.	"I will come back and take you to be with me" (John 14:3).
29.	I'll never worship Jesus Christ.	29.	"Every knee should bow...and every tongue confess that Jesus Christ is Lord" (Phil. 2:10–11).
30.	All religions are basically the same.	30.	"Salvation is found in no one else, for there is no other name under heaven given to men by which we must be saved" (Acts 4:12).

190

THIS IS A GENERATION POISED FOR A REVOLUTION

As you can see, authentic Christianity is countercultural to the ways of the world. But as the world watches the kingdom of God in action through the lives of authentic Christians, they will be challenged by not merely a meeting but a movement inaugurated by Jesus Himself!

Some Christians look at the current generation of youth and remark that it is a "dead generation." They would find it hard to imagine a movement of authentic Christianity beginning with today's youth. But let me state emphatically that I believe God is sending an "Elijah ministry" today, just as He promised.

The first account in Scripture of a person raised from the dead was a fatherless young man (like so many today!) who was resurrected by Elijah. (See 1 Kings 17.) The second person raised from the dead in Scripture was a young man with an indifferent father (like so many today!), resurrected by Elijah's disciple, Elisha. (See 2 Kings 4.)

To those who lament pessimistically that God can't raise up a seemingly "dead" generation of young people, I say, "Open your eyes and look at the fields! They are ripe for harvest" (John 4:35). The Elijah generation of spiritual revolutionaries is emerging!

God is birthing a revolution that is bringing two generations together for God's glory just as He promised in the closing verses of the Old Testament.

> See, I will send you the prophet Elijah before that great and dreadful day of the LORD comes. He will

191

> turn the hearts of the fathers to their children, and
> the hearts of the children to their fathers; or else I
> will come and strike the land with a curse.
> —MALACHI 4:5–6

The Bible records two generations that Satan sought to destroy—largely because of their great potential for a righteous revolution. When God was raising up Moses as a spiritual revolutionary, Satan incited Pharaoh to destroy scores of little ones in a vain attempt to thwart a mighty move of God. (See Exodus 1.) Centuries later when God sent Jesus to revolutionize history, Satan again, through Herod, viciously attacked a generation to frustrate the plan of God. (See Matthew 2.)

Today, God is raising up another revolutionary generation. They don't bomb abortion clinics, bash gays or blow up schools. This generation is composed of adults and youth who give themselves "by life or by death" (Phil. 1:20) to holiness, humility and the uncompromising, life-changing gospel of Jesus Christ.

192   Could it be that Satan, "filled with fury, because he knows his time is short" (Rev. 12:12), sees what lies on the horizon? Could he be attempting to obliterate a generation through whom God's purpose will ultimately be fulfilled? Yet as Satan tried and failed on two previous occasions, he will fail once again as the true people of God emerge at the end of this age!

A rendezvous with destiny awaits this multigenerational movement of pioneers as the stage is set for a final duel. It's a contest between the armies of two super gladiators—God and Satan—the latter having already received his sentence of defeat.

SEVEN UNIQUE CHARACTERISTICS OF THIS GENERATION OF YOUTH

The characteristics and needs of the current generation of young people are unique and unlike any other in recent history. Not since the first century has a generation in Western culture been so unacquainted with the institutional church. But that's good. Young people who have no "baggage" from the traditional church will identify with the power of authentic Christianity.

Understanding youth culture will enable you to pray much more effectively as God draws the fathers and children together. Here are seven characteristics of youth culture that I believe positions young people to fulfill the declarations of Malachi 4:5–6.

Characteristic #1: Youth are uncomfortable with the institutional church.

Many young people today are like the crippled man in Acts 3:

193

> One day Peter and John were going up to the temple at the time of prayer—at three in the afternoon. Now a man crippled from birth was being carried to the temple gate called Beautiful, where he was put every day to beg from those going into the temple courts.
>
> —ACTS 3:1–2

Pushed to the margins of society by his infirmity, the crippled man was forced to beg outside the temple courts. Jaded and lethargic from the humiliation of his "trade," he simply wanted release from his physical condition. Obviously, people passed him by every day on the way to the temple courts, yet he still felt set apart and isolated from them.

In the same way, the younger unchurched generation feels "different" from most people in the church. The music and jargon inside is so unlike their own that they perceive Christianity as irrelevant. Although interested in Jesus, their meager spiritual condition and the awkwardness of entering a church forces them to sit outside—by the temple gates.

Characteristic #2: They have been enmeshed in our high-tech culture.

This is the first generation to grow up in the "wired for light and sound" whirlwind of electronic wizardry. They are surrounded—and dependent upon—lightning-fast computers, high-tech DVD players, high-definition televisions, satellite dishes and video games, which grasp today's teens with ever-extending tentacles.

No wonder the attention span of young people is short—ask any junior high or high school teacher. The "prince of the power of the air" (Eph. 2:2, NKJV) is exploiting these technological advances to mold the masses after his designs.

Characteristic #3: This generation has lost its innocence.

Many children today are prematurely thrust from childhood into adulthood. In the absence of a stable family structure, many face major moral decisions before they're prepared to make them: "Should I smoke dope?" "Should I sleep with him?" "Should I get an abortion?" They also face a lifetime of consequences due to their ill-informed and premature decisions.

194

Characteristic #4: They are coping with the repercussions of the breakup of the traditional family.

Many young people lack the supportive base of a stable family. One in every five children lives in a single-parent household—what used to be called a "broken home." Even the definition of "family" has been broadened to include alternative lifestyles. Homosexual couples are now allowed to marry and adopt children. The traditional nuclear family (dad works and mom stays home with the kids) has become the exception rather than the rule, abandoning this young generation to face enormous challenges without adequate parental support.

Characteristic #5: They are exposed to pornography.

Exposure to pornography and perversion among young people is unprecedented. Computers and cable television make the availability of pornography a fact of life. MSNBC recently stated that out of 57 million Internet subscribers in January 2000, 25 million spent an average of ten hours weekly at porn sites. That's almost half of the people who use the Internet!

These are mainly adults—right? Not quite. A recent study conducted by the *NetValue Report on Minors* found that people under seventeen spend more time surfing adult-oriented sites than they do game or other entertainment sites. Over one recent month, 27.5 percent of all minors surfing the Internet visited an adult site.

Characteristic #6: This generation is polluted by music.

Equally alarming is this generation's primary medium of expression—music. Rock and roll, as immoral as it was, has deteriorated into perverted "hip-hop" and "porn rock." One performer in particular, Eminem, was nominated for a 2001 Best Album Grammy that depicted rape, murder and perversion.

Many parents are ignorant of these preachers of perversion who masquerade as musicians. But music is far from harmless. "Music is a spiritual thing of its own," rock star Jimi Hendrix reportedly once said. "You can hypnotize with music, and when you get people at their weakest point you can preach into the subconscious what you want to say." Obviously, Hendrix's prophetic words are being fulfilled.

Characteristic #7: They are morally neutered.

This is the first morally neutered generation in American history! In the name of "separation of church and state" and "tolerance," schools are teaching youth that absolutes do not exist. Abortion is a personal choice; homosexuality is an alternative lifestyle; and premarital sex is healthy and good.

Judeo-Christian values that shaped people's lives for centuries have eroded in a single generation. Tolerance (based on absolutes derived from Judeo-Christian Scriptures) used to mean that people were given the right to believe differently. Today "tolerance" means everyone must accept another person's beliefs—unless, of course, that person believes in absolute truth.

196

THE TIME IS RIPE FOR ANOTHER REVOLUTION

Having exhausted the sin spectrum, today's youth are now in God's "cross hairs" for a righteous revolution. Just as God awaited the "fullness of time" to send a Redeemer, He's about to send rain from heaven, because "the fields" of today's young generation "are white unto harvest."

God is poised for intervention. He is stirring the hearts of a generation of adults and youth who will blaze a new trail. And their message of revolution will rescue the masses, in a way similar to Vaclav Maly's experience in Czechoslovakia. Psalm 110:3 speaks prophetically of this day: "Your troops will be willing on your day of battle. Arrayed in holy majesty, from the womb of the dawn you will receive the dew of your *youth***" (emphasis added).**

The gathering of three hundred thousand parents and youth on the Mall in Washington, D.C. (The Call D.C., held September 2, 2000) for prayer, fasting and marching orders represents the first installment of a new "velvet revolution."

A few months later, a Christian president was elected whose first act was to cut off funding for overseas abortions. George W. Bush's presidential inauguration was a prophetic picture to the world of the next move of God—multigenerational ministry. At his inauguration, a father and son—a current and former president—sat side by side on the same platform for the first time in U.S. history!

197

FOUR KEYS THAT WILL BRING TOGETHER THE YOUNG AND OLD FOR MULTIGENERATIONAL MINISTRY

God is poised for the greatest revolutionary revival among young people in history.

> In the last days, God says, I will pour out my Spirit
> on all people. Your sons and daughters will
> prophesy, your young men will see visions, your
> old men will dream dreams.
>
> —ACTS 2:17

He has allowed an entire generation to be led out to
the precipice of disaster in order to fulfill Malachi's
prophecy that the hearts of the fathers would turn to
their children and the hearts of the children would
turn to their fathers.

Having examined what makes this generation unique
from any other in history, here are four keys to help us
bridge the gap between the two generations.

1. Issue a bold challenge.

When Peter and John encountered the crippled man
in Acts 3, they issued a bold challenge: "Look at us!"
Many youth today are confused because parents, schools
and society fail to give them a bold challenge. Deep
inside, youth want the security that leadership and
absolute truth provide. When people lament that this is
a directionless, apathetic generation, boldly declare to
them, "This is the way, walk ye in it" (Isa. 30:21, KJV).

Young people are seeking a cause bigger than themselves. Like the baby-boomer activism of the '60s and
the countercultural revolution that launched the historic Jesus People movement, this generation wants to
know that their lives make a difference.

Many leaders mistakenly assume the only way to
relate to youth is by sugarcoating the gospel's call for
total commitment. By providing entertainment,
movies and games, they think they're doing "ministry."
But they're not.

Students need to be challenged to live out an uncompromising, radical commitment to Jesus Christ. They need to see themselves as agents of God's righteous revolution to alter the destiny of nations. Jesus' instructions are clear. "Any of you who does not give up everything he has cannot be my disciple" (Luke 14:33).

Adults embracing the role of spiritual fathers and mothers must be bold in inviting young people to join them in this intergenerational, spiritual revolution. Make a difference in this generation by exhorting young people—and others—to fulfill their personal, God-given destinies. Dismantle the stereotype many have of ministry that says God reserves only a select few for His work. Instead, present them with unlimited opportunities that invade every facet of society with the liberating gospel message.

2. Provide personal involvement.

For an uncompromising message to be issued, mentors will be needed. Young people need to count the cost of laying down their lives for the gospel, but adults will need to lay down their lives also by investing their time in mentoring relationships.

In Acts 3, Peter and John demonstrated another key to bridging the gap with today's youth. Although multitudes passed the crippled man sitting at the temple gate, Peter gave more than the other people's token coins: *"Taking him by the right hand,* he helped him up, and instantly the man's feet and ankles became strong" (Acts 3:7, emphasis added).

Token youth ministry that merely keeps young people busy is not enough. Considering the depth of their need, youth must be discipled and welcomed into a

199

spiritual family, not merely given a youth group or Sunday morning service to attend.

Young people who are the product of broken families need relationships in the context of a strong local church where they can derive the love, ongoing support and guidance they need. Spiritual dads and moms are important in mentoring them to maturity.

Many young girls have given themselves over to sexual immorality because they lack genuine love at home. Many young men have become ensnared by homosexuality as a result of a lack of healthy fatherly affection. Many teenagers have taken their lives because they felt that no one really cares.

You can *impress* people from a distance, but you will *impact* them when you involve yourself in their lives. You teach what you know, but you impart who you are! And that takes place only through relationships.

Make an intentional effort to involve yourself and your church in the youth culture. Make youth outreach a priority—first of all for you as an individual, and then in your local church. If you are a pastor, don't merely preach it from your pulpit—also make it a priority item in the church budget. Disciple, affirm and spend time with your young people and youth pastor. Participate in specific youth events, publicly recognize your youth group's projects and accomplishments and tailor your sermons to encompass youth as well as adults. Look for ways to honor and showcase them in spheres of ministry like worship teams, intercession and evangelism.

If you are not a pastor, support the youth ministry in your church with your time—and your money. Invite young people to your home, mentor them and volunteer

200

your time and talents with their projects. Pray for the young people you know, and become actively involved in outreach events and opportunities to reach the unchurched youth in your community. Be there for them when they need you. Make multigenerational ministry a reality, not a fantasy, in your church!

Another key to unite the two generations in effective ministry is...

3. Offer relevant worship.

Authentic worship must be recaptured and demonstrated as a celebration rather than a ceremony.

After reaching out his hand to the crippled man in Acts 3, Peter pulled the man to his feet, and he was healed. What was the man's response? "He jumped to his feet and began to walk. Then he went with them into the temple courts, walking and jumping, and praising God" (Acts 3:8). Rather than repress his God-given emotions, he praised God with exuberance.

Few things appeal to a young person more than music. The primary target of the music industry is obvious: young people.

Why are young people so drawn to the world's brand of music and often so "turned off" by what they've experienced in the church? Could it be that in their youthful exuberance they long to express themselves in creative forms that are upbeat, dynamic and pulsating with life? Unfortunately, more often than not they find church music somber, predictable and devoid of life.

Worship of Jehovah was not always this way. When King David restored the tabernacle as the center of Jewish worship and culture, he secured "singers, with instruments of music, harps, lyres, loud-sounding cymbals, to raise sounds of joy" (1 Chron. 15:16, NAS).

Today, Satan's musical conspiracy is being exposed as the counterfeit to true worship. The tabernacle of David is being restored "in order that the rest of mankind [including young people] may seek the Lord" (Acts 15:17, NAS).

It's time to leave behind dead religion, kick off your shoes and engage yourself in pulsating praise and wonderful worship for the glory of God!

4. Demonstrate supernatural ministry.

> When all the people saw him walking and praising God, they recognized him as the same man who used to sit begging...and they were filled with wonder and amazement at what had happened to him.
>
> —ACTS 3:9–10

After the supernatural power of God was released in the crippled man's life, the people's hearts were open to hearing the gospel. At that point, Peter and John preached powerfully to the people, and the news of their preaching reached even the Sanhedrin.

If you are wondering how the masses of young people are going to be reached in these last days, look no further. God is returning His people to the original method of attracting the multitudes—a mighty display of His presence and power!

Our emotionally scarred, burned-out, sexually abused youth culture needs to experience the miraculous power and manifest presence of almighty God. These masses of lethargic, passive, causeless young people need to be jolted out of their complacency so they will become world-changers rather than life-drifters.

A miraculous breakthrough was needed to transform the people in Elijah's day from onlookers who "said nothing" into believers who fell on their faces and cried out, "The LORD—he is God! The LORD—he is God!" (1 Kings 18:21, 39). The same is already happening today.

As I travel the United States and abroad, I am beginning to witness a rapid increase in the number and intensity of signs and wonders. A while ago while ministering in England, I watched the power of God fall on four thousand people who were delivered from debilitating sins (sexual sins, drugs and cigarettes). Hundreds received physical healings, and well over one hundred young people responded to the call to follow the living God.

One young man was so excited upon hearing a supernatural word of knowledge concerning his back injury (which also resulted in his healing) that he literally picked me up amidst the cheering crowd and carried me around the stage!

203

As the climax of the age draws near, God is initiating a righteous revolution that will reach a needy world. A multigenerational army of spiritual pioneers is emerging to hasten Christ's return. Spiritual fathers and mothers are colaboring with this younger generation to see Jesus exalted, His church built in authenticity and a needy world reached with the gospel in declaration and demonstration.

A righteous revolution has begun that will rock the world. Will you respond to the call?

Thirteen

Taking Action and Living Adventurously

The adventure novel is a growing market in publishing. Millions of adventure books are sold each year, telling riveting stories of pioneers and adventurers. Whether climbing Mount Everest as a blind person or snowshoeing alone across the North Pole, readers just can't seem to get enough.

But would you consider those readers of adventure novels to be pioneers and adventurers? Of course not. Not unless they become pioneers and adventurers themselves. The world is filled with armchair pioneers who dream of throwing caution to the wind and embarking on an adventure with reckless abandon. But because they never leave their recliners, they aren't pioneers.

The same is true of spiritual pioneers in the kingdom of God. Paul wrote, "For the kingdom of God is not a matter of talk but of power" (1 Cor. 4:20). You can talk about being a pioneer, but until you take action it is only talk. In fact, taking action is a sign of truly knowing God. "The people who know their God will display strength and take action" (Dan. 11:32, NAS).

204

The God you and I serve is a God of activity and action, not passivity and stagnation. He calls His people to renounce passive living in order to be catalysts for righteousness within their cultures. Jesus commands His people to pick up their cross—not their television remote control—and follow Him "to do good works, which God prepared in advance for [them] to do" (Eph. 2:10).

While some perceive Christianity as a leisure cruise to Gloryland, the real picture of the faith is a revolutionary army of explorers who "boldly go where no man has gone before." Jesus Christ calls His radical, End-Time revolutionaries to be world changers, not time wasters, and to be people of action, not people of inactivity.

> They will be my people, and I will be their God. I will give them singleness of heart and *action*, so that they will always fear me for their own good and the good of their children after them.
> —JEREMIAH 32:38–39, EMPHASIS ADDED

> In the same way, faith by itself, if it is not accompanied by *action,* is dead.
> —JAMES 2:17, EMPHASIS ADDED

205

Christianity that lacks action lacks adventure and is perceived as cold, lifeless and boring. My friend and Bible teacher Terry Virgo tells of a newly saved young man who, seeing a church nearby, sadly asked, "Now that I'm a Christian, do I have to go into that building?" A common cry against religion goes up from today's youth: "I want action, not boredom!"

And God couldn't agree more! The days ahead are

destined to be days of *action*! Jesus did not give the Holy Spirit to His followers for personal blessing, but for power—that they might take the gospel to the ends of the earth. He also gave His Holy Spirit to empower His people to live holy lives—presented as the spotless bride at the end of the age.

Before you lies the most dynamic phase in church history. The outpouring of the Holy Spirit in the twentieth century, the spread of Christianity around the world and the advent of church planting and church-centered leadership development all point to the culmination of the end of the age.

To succeed in this final initiative, God is impressing upon Christians worldwide to rid themselves of meaningless religious ritual. At the same time He is infusing them with aggressive, godly ambition—to love Jesus passionately and to see the true church of Jesus Christ emerge in the earth!

For too long Christians have been over-equipped and under-challenged. Now is the time to make your move in the kingdom of God. After all, Jesus said, "The kingdom of heaven suffers violence, and violent men take it by force" (Matt. 11:12, NAS).

206

TAKING ACTION MEANS TAKING RISKS

Don't run the risk of growing old dreaming of what could have been. Your biography is being written one day at a time. At the end of the age, you don't want to be bored reading your own life story when it could have been an adventure novel. God has called you to live adventurously!

Helen Keller, though blind and deaf from age two, refused to be overcome by her disability. Rather than retreating into the darkness of her world, she ambitiously pursued her dreams. "Security is mostly a superstition. It does not exist in nature, nor do the children of men as a whole experience it," she commented. "Avoiding danger is no safer in the long run than outright exposure. *Life is either a daring adventure, or nothing.*"

Did you get that? Life is either a daring adventure, or nothing.

But what if I step out in some area and make a mistake? I'm afraid I'll fail.

God is more pleased when you step out and make mistakes than when you sit back and do nothing for fear of failure! You cannot please God when you try to avoid making mistakes. "Without faith it is impossible to please God" (Heb. 11:6). Best of all, God is more than able to redeem your mistakes.

John Grisham, one of the most successful novelists today (with more than one hundred million books in print in thirty-one languages), was rejected by twenty-eight agents and editors before finally landing a publisher for his first novel. And of his first initial printing of five thousand copies, he purchased one thousand himself and peddled them from the trunk of his car.

But had he decided not to take action or to live adventurously, he would still be a small town lawyer.

Emerging on the earth is a new generation of pioneers who are captivated by God and His purposes. Arising out of their intimate relationship with Him is a determination to take action and to live adventurously!

207

Only one question remains. Will you join the ranks of the spiritual pioneers who, with reckless abandon, have gone before you and who, hopefully, will follow in your footsteps? To conclude this chapter I offer some suggestions to take the next step.

TAKING ACTION AS PIONEERS

As you launch out as a spiritual pioneer, certain spiritual habits will enable you to become a man or woman of action:

Personal devotions

Intimacy with God is essential if you want to challenge the status quo. The Ephesian Christians, while praised for their spiritual activity, grieved God for abandoning their simple "first love" devotion to him (Rev. 2:1–6).

If you feel spiritually dry, you probably need a second honeymoon with the Lord. By rekindling your personal relationship with Him through prayer and time in His Word, you will recapture the zeal and enthusiasm that accompanies newborn faith. Remember that intimacy precedes ministry!

Lifestyle evangelism

Loneliness plagues modern society. As people feel rejected, exploited and wounded, they retreat into themselves. Though they may resist the thought of religion, they are much more likely to respond to a call to a relationship. Jesus provides the ultimate example of the friend of sinners (Luke 7:34). He didn't care how unclean they were from leprosy or sin. Jesus loved them and accepted them. His followers should do no less.

Gifts of the Spirit

Computers, DVDs, CDs and high-tech video games are no match for a supernatural demonstration of the living God. In a society that is searching for something beyond the five senses, the gifts of the Spirit transport you into a dimension that flesh and blood cannot overcome.

Paul exhorted the Corinthians to "eagerly desire spiritual gifts" (1 Cor. 14:1). God will never refuse His gifts to those who actively seek them! Now is the time to give expression to any impression that the Spirit gives you.

Practical service

"We are God's workmanship, created in Christ Jesus to do good works, which God prepared in advance for us to do" (Eph. 2:10). Opportunities for practical service are all around you. Your job is to recognize and respond. Love in action—meals delivered to the family that just moved in next door; assistance for widows, orphans and the sick—will totally amaze a cynical world. Rely on God's strength and creative direction as you make yourself a servant to all.

Prophetic social action

As the "salt of the earth," Christians are commissioned to preserve righteousness and prevent moral decay. While society teaches people to look the other way, Christians must be people of compassionate conviction who pray, fast and courageously speak out for the cause of righteousness. Christians should be leading the way in opposing pornography, abortion and neglect of the poor and oppressed.

Divine healing

Whether faced with a common cold or an inability to conceive children, you serve the God who heals—so take action! God answers faith-filled prayers both to bless His people and to confirm the power of the gospel. Avoid merely throwing out a "God bless you" to those in need—seize the opportunity and pray!

Resist the demonic

Christians often let the enemy beat them down without even putting up a fight. When you can identify an obvious demonic root to a problem, resolve yourself to resist the heaviness, the lingering condemnation or the unexplainable lust. "No weapon forged against you will prevail, and you will refute every tongue that accuses you. This is the heritage of the servants of the LORD" (Isa. 54:17).

LIVING ADVENTUROUSLY AS PIONEERS

As you make a lifestyle out of taking action, you are primed to live adventurously as a spiritual pioneer. Here are some ideas to help you on your way.

210

Join a church planting team.

Prayerfully consider involving yourself with an apostolic church planting team that serves as the nucleus for establishing a New Testament church. It's never too late!

Explore opportunities for short-term evangelism.

Investigate the possibilities of joining a church-based team that will expand your horizons in another city or culture. Go as an adult or go as a young adult. Just go. You'll never be the same!

Participate in world missions.

As God is fulfilling the Great Commission through domestic and crosscultural church planting ventures, opportunities are surfacing for training and service that will bear "fruit that remains." Have you sensed that you should evangelize in other lands such as Central America, Asia, Europe and Africa, yet neglected the call? By all means, *don't let the flame die out!*

Invest your finances to fulfill the Great Commission.

God desires to underwrite the Great Commission through generous Christians who give over and above their normal tithes and offerings to the church. Proven ministries that extend the kingdom of God through church planting, leadership development and the proclamation of a current word from God need your partnership in both prayer and financial giving. The promise holds true: "Whoever sows sparingly will also reap sparingly, and whoever sows generously will also reap generously" (2 Cor. 9:6).

Pursue further biblical training.

Consider enrolling in an internship program at a local church, specialized "equippers" seminars/conferences or as a part-time or full-time student in an anointed Bible school. Deepen your understanding of the Word of God so you can apply it in the arena of life.

Find an authentic New Testament church.

If you're languishing in a lifeless situation—identified in 2 Timothy 3:5 as "having a form of godliness but denying its power"—maybe it's time to graciously, yet courageously, heed the counsel given in the next line: "Have nothing to do with them." Expect flak for not "blooming where you're planted," but if you're obeying the Holy Spirit in a right attitude, He'll more than amply provide for you! Get "planted" in a church where people pursue God, honor the Scriptures 100 percent and take seriously the call to live out genuine New Testament Christianity.

Come out of self-imposed retirement from local church life.

The most subtle, yet most dangerous, form of worldliness is allowing the twin gods of society—comfort and convenience—to lure you out of active service in Christ's kingdom. Beware of seemingly legitimate reasons. "I'm not as young as I used to be." "I have a family now." "There's too much to do around the house." "Let others have their turn." "I've got lots to do with school...my job...my career."

The "you deserve a break today" mentality has seduced the Western church at a time when God is calling for a new ruthlessness in dealing with self-indulgent tendencies. If you've noticed a loss of your radical edge, now is the time to rouse yourself from a Laodicean slumber and recommit your time, talents and treasure to things of eternal value. (See Revelation 3:14–22.)

212

Obviously this list is just the beginning. Ask the Holy Spirit to guide you into your next steps, and He will answer you!

Twenty years after my high school graduation, I decided to return to my old stomping grounds to reminisce and see how things had changed. Driving through my old neighborhood, I was flooded with memories—some good and some not so good.

My mind raced back to the rock band I had played in at that time—ironically named The Lost Souls. Another member of the band—my best friend—later died a tragic, alcohol-related death. How I wished he had known Jesus! But how could I have shared the Good News when I was still a lost soul at the time?

After surveying the neighborhood, my driving eventually led me to the familiar Big Boy Restaurant where I had spent countless hours after many events at school.

Once inside I noticed how the years had taken their toll on the interior of the restaurant. Flashbacks of bygone gatherings and faces were swirling through my head, when suddenly I noticed an unkempt yet familiar fellow from my high school days seated at the counter. Immediately he recognized me, too! Within seconds we were exchanging pleasantries and high fives as we sat down at the wobbly table to stroll down memory lane.

"So, John, do you see many of the guys from our class anymore?" I asked.

"Eh, sometimes. I think most of the dudes from our class ended up in one of four places." Taking a sip from my straw, I looked up, curious as to what he'd say.

"I may be off," he began, "but most of the guys are either on drugs and divorced, some are in jail, a bunch are already dead and then there's another batch that have become those 'born-again' Christians."

His assessment was obviously exaggerated and a bit sarcastic, but the last grouping caught my attention. I chuckled as I leaned back on my chair.

John then shared how he had been busted for drugs and was trying to get his life back together by coaching athletics at an elementary school down the street. He was still strung out on dope although he wanted to be set free. When I inquired about the reality of God in his life, he responded, "I'm really not sure anymore if He exists."

Before leaving the restaurant, I made sure John had my personal tract in hand. As I drove by the restaurant window, I couldn't help shedding a tear as I saw the slumped-over, stubble-faced shell of a man, now puffing his cigarette as he perched once again at the counter.

"The mass of humanity live lives of quiet desperation," wrote Henry Thoreau. Jesus said, "I came that they might have life, and might have it abundantly" (John 10:10, NAS).

You likely have friends who, like John, live lives of quiet desperation. Rich or poor, single, divorced or married, they spend their lives searching to fill the void that only Jesus can fill.

My driving passion is to see every lost soul like John throughout this nation and abroad encounter the real Jesus and authentic New Testament Christianity. This is not merely my message—it's my mission in life. **Where people have known religion, God longs for them to discover reality and relationship. Where people experience bondage, He intends for them to find liberation. God wants humanity to encounter the Jesus of the Bible, the One who is "the same yesterday and today and forever" (Heb. 13:8). They may not all accept Him, but they should have a chance to at least reject Him based upon witnessing the *real* thing.**

The church hasn't always done a good job of introducing people to the real Jesus, but the restoration of God's church *will* happen. Authentic Christianity is emerging. His kingdom *will* come, and His will *will* be done. The question is: Will you choose to join Him in His work?

"See, I am doing a new thing!" God says (Isa. 43:19). Well, the new thing begins with spiritual pioneers who are recklessly abandoned to God. They are revolutionary men and women—young and older together—who willingly take risks because they know the harvest is great but the workers are few.

Please don't settle for status quo Christianity, because the time is short. In these climactic hours, God is beginning a new wave of revival, restoration and spiritual

215

revolution. He desires to show the world that He cares, that He is able to do today what He accomplished through Jesus' earthly ministry and the early church. He wants to demonstrate a gospel of power that is accompanied by signs and wonders, and He wants to prepare His bride for His return.

It is no mistake that God has allowed you to be alive during this critical juncture. You have been given a front row seat to witness the finale of the greatest action drama in history. But God doesn't want you sitting in the front row—*He wants you to join the drama.*

Will you be one of the spiritual pioneers who dare to believe God to use you to reach your generation with a declaration of an authentic gospel message and demonstration of an authentic New Testament church?

If your reply is a resounding "Yes!" then the heart of a pioneer is in you!

With reckless abandon will you respond to the same challenge given me almost thirty years ago?

"If you would do the best with your life, find out what God is doing in your generation—and fling yourself into it."

216

Chapter 1
Tomorrow's Man

1. R. T. Kendall, *The Anointing: Three Eras* (London: Hodder and Stoughton, 1999), ix.
2. Ibid., quoting Jim Bakker in the Foreword, xiv.

Chapter 2
Constant Change Is Here to Stay

1. John Ayto, *Dictionary of Word Origins* (New York: Arcade Publishing, 1990), s.v. *pioneer.*
2. Ibid., s.v. *settle.*
3. Deuteronomy 1:2 says, "It takes eleven days to go from Horeb to Kadesh Barnea by the Mount Seir road." Is this not one of the Bible's saddest verses?
4. Source obtained from the Internet: www.pbs.org/wgbh/pages/frontline/president/players/sculley.html.

Chapter 4
Restoration: It Will Happen!

1. Sadly enough, the same pattern is repeated today among some Anabaptists who resist people in their congregations or fellow churches that embrace new moves of the Spirit. However, this resistance isn't limited only to Anabaptist churches.

Chapter 6
How to Really Know Jesus

1. *Dictionary of Jesus and the Gospels*, eds. Joel G. Green, Scot McKnight, I. Howard Marshall (Downer's Grove, IL: InterVarsity Press, 1998, 1992), s.v. *Historical Jesus, Quest of.*

217

Chapter 7
Real Revival

1. *The Theological Dictionary of the New Testament,* abridged in one volume, eds. Gerhard Kittel, and Gerhard Friedrich (Grand Rapids, MI: William B. Eerdmans Publishing Co., 1985), s.v. *anapsyxis.*

2. Ibid., s.v. *chairo*.

3. Kendall, *The Anointing: Three Eras.*

Chapter 9
The Pursuit of Humility

1. W. E. Vine, Merrill F. Unger and William White, *Vine's Complete Expository Dictionary of Old and New Testament Words* (Nashville, TN: Thomas Nelson, 1997), s.v. *resist.*

2. Billy Graham, *Just As I Am* (New York: HarperCollins, 1997), xii.

Chapter 10
Authentic Christianity

1. I am indebted to Pastor Rick Warren for this distinction of understanding between church growth and church health. He further explains in his book *The Purpose-Driven Church* (Grand Rapids, MI: Zondervan, 1996).

2. H. G. and Scott Liddell, *Abridged Greek-English Lexicon* (Oxford: Oxford University Press, 1992), s.v. "orge."

3. William MacDonald, *True Discipleship* (Kansas City, KS: Walterick Publications, expanded edition 1975).

4. Amos 9:11.

5. For a closer look at the changes David instituted, read 1 Chronicles 15 and 16.

6. A good example of a hymn from the New Testament church is Philippians 2:6–11.

Chapter 11
Radical or Simply Biblical?

1. Walter Bauer, F. Wilbur Gingrich and Frederick W. Danker, *A Greek-English Lexicon of the New Testament and Other Early Christian Literature,* (Chicago: University of Chicago Press, 1979), s.v. *proskartereo.*

2. It is important to note that Ephesians 4:11–13 is an explanation of the offices in the church—people who are gifts to the church—which varies slightly from gifts given to people.

3. A lengthy explanation of the various spiritual gifts lies

beyond the scope of this book. A good resource for learning more about spiritual gifts is *Discover Your Spiritual Gifts* by C. Peter Wagner. (Ventura, CA: Regal Book, 2002). Wagner also offers a spiritual gifts inventory entitled *Finding Your Spiritual Gifts* (Ventura, CA: Regal Books, 1995).

4. A good book on money and tithing that I highly recommend is *Money, Possessions, and Eternity* by Randy Alcorn (Wheaton, IL: Tyndale House, 1989).

5. Two passages of Scripture come to mind that help in dealing with conflict. Matthew 18:15–17 provides a good pattern to follow, and Acts 6:1–7 provides an excellent example of how the early believers dealt with conflict and how God blessed them as a result.

Characteristics of an Authentic New Testament Church

1. Jesus Christ is exalted as the Son of God who is risen from the dead (Acts 22–24).

2. The Bible is honored and taught as God's revealed will for His creation (2 Tim. 3:16–17).

3. Freedom and vitality are expressed during corporate praise and worship (Col. 3:16; Ps. 150).

4. Genuine love is shared between the people (John 13:34–35).

5. Interpersonal relationships are built that go beyond attendance at meetings and services (Acts 2:42–47; 5:42).

6. The leaders encourage pastoral care that ministers to the whole person—body, mind and spirit (Acts 2:44–45).

7. The leaders exemplify Christian virtue (integrity, loyalty, humility) and not merely personality, showmanship and speaking ability (1 Tim. 3:1–13).

8. The fivefold ministry gifts (apostles, prophets, pastors, evangelists and teachers) are allowed to operate, which in turn equip the people for works of service and ground them in biblical maturity (Eph. 4:11–15).

9. The congregation believes in and practices biblical spiritual authority (Heb. 13:17).

10. The church has an evangelistic, outward thrust that reaches others with the good news of Jesus Christ (Matt. 28:19–20).

11. Conflict is handled biblically (Matt. 18:15–18).

12. People's lives are positively changed through their involvement with the church (Acts 4:31).

The Thirty "One Anothers" of New Testament Christianity

—Compiled by Larry Tomczak

- Love one another—John 13:34
- Mutually depend on one another—Acts 2:40–46
- Be devoted to one another—Romans 12:10
- Outdo one another in showing honor—Romans 12:9
- Rejoice with one another—Romans 12:14
- Weep with one another—Romans 12:14
- Have the same mind toward one another—Romans 12:16
- Don't judge one another—Romans 14:3
- Accept one another—Romans 15:7
- Counsel one another—Romans 15:14
- Greet one another—Romans 16:16
- Wait for one another—1 Corinthians 11:32
- Care for one another—1 Corinthians 12:25
- Serve one another—Galatians 5:13
- Bear one another's burdens—Galatians 6:2
- Be kind to one another—Ephesians 4:24
- Forgive one another—Ephesians 4:24
- Submit to one another—Ephesians 5:21
- Forbear with one another—Ephesians 4:2
- Encourage one another—Hebrews 3:13
- Build up one another—1 Thessalonians 5:11
- Stir up one another—Hebrews 10:24

223

- Be hospitable to one another—1 Peter 4:9
- Minister gifts to one another—1 Peter 4:9
- Be clothed in humility to one another—1 Peter 5:5
- Don't speak evil against one another—Titus 3:2
- Don't grumble against one another—James 5:8
- Confess your faults to one another—James 5:16
- Pray for one another—James 5:16
- Fellowship with one another—1 John 1:7

A Comparison of Traditional and Biblical Models of a Local Church

Category	Traditional Model	Biblical Model
1. Concept of church	Organization (much like a "club" or "lodge")	Organism (with organization) but seen as the living body of Christ (1 Cor. 12:27)
2. Head	The people	Jesus Christ (Col. 1:18)
3. Authority	Constitution plus "proof-texts" from the Bible	The whole Word of God (2 Tim. 3:16–17)
4. Believers	"Members" (as in a club); "attenders" at a service	Disciples (disciplined ones) and brothers/sisters (integral parts of a spiritual family) (Eph. 2:19)
5. Involvement	Spectators	Participants (1 Cor. 12:27)
6. Government	Democracy (of the people, by the people, etc.)	Theocracy (God leading through the Word and the Holy Spirit) (Col. 1:18)

225

CATEGORY	TRADITIONAL MODEL	BIBLICAL MODEL
7. Selection of leadership	Recruit a "professional," gauge his preaching, hire him for a job	Divine appointment (depending on God to raise up gifted leaders) (Eph. 4:11)
8. Basic ministry	Preach sermons and conduct services	Glorify God by equipping people to fulfill a mission (Eph. 4:12)
9. Place of ministry	Church building (at stated times)	Church facility, homes, in the marketplace—all the time (Acts 2:46)
10. Primary concerns	Attract the people with whatever works	Glorify God and obey His Word (John 15:9–10)
11. Objectives	Buildings, bucks, bodies and breaking attendance records	Follow the biblical pattern to build up the body (Eph. 4:11–16) and reach the world with the gospel
12. Determining factor	What the people want (peace at any price)	What God declares and the people need (2 Tim. 4:2–3)
13. Great Commission	Get converts (addition)	Make disciples (multiplication) (Matt. 28:19)
14. Field	The immediate vicinity	The world (Matt. 28:19)
15. Purpose of assembling	Conduct services and programs.	Become a dwelling place for God's presence through prayer, worship, breaking bread, applying His Word, ministering His gifts and stirring each other to love and good deeds (Heb. 10:24)

Category	Traditional Model	Biblical Model
16. Attitude while assembled	"Will I get out on time?"	"God, I've gathered with You and Your people. Speak to my heart; change me; equip me; use me." (1 Pet. 2:2)
17. Material presented	Whatever makes people feel good and keeps them coming back	Hearing and applying a current word from God (James 1:22)
18. Emphasis	Gathering people (quantity)	Growth in godliness (quality and quantity) (1 Tim. 4:7)
19. Leadership	A one-man ministry that exists to meet his every need	Apostles, prophets, evangelists, pastors and teachers (fivefold ministry) who equip the people for works of service (Eph. 4:11–12)
20. Leadership model	Minister "hired" to do a job the way the board deems fit	Team of leaders (with one primary leader) who seek God and lead the flock as Scripture directs (1 Pet. 5:1–3)
21. Church discipline	Nonexistent	An expression of God's love (Heb. 12:10) and part of safeguarding God's flock (Acts 20:28)
22. Deakonate	Subtly and indirectly control the church and keep leaders in line.	Handle the practical needs of the church so ministers can "give themselves to the ministry of the Word and prayer" (Acts 6)

Category	Traditional Model	Biblical Model
23. Resources	Human ingenuity, "business, techniques" and available funds	The Word, prayer, Holy Spirit, spiritual gifts, wise counsel (2 Pet. 1:3)
24. Methodology	"That's the way we've always done it."	Message and mandate fixed, methods flexible (2 Tim. 4:2–4)
25. Procedures	Plead, pressure and project guilt	Teach God's Word and trust Him to raise up gifted individuals for the task at hand (Eph. 4:15–16)
26. Leadership given to…	Anyone willing	Called, anointed, godly, faithful, proven servants (1 Tim. 3:1–6)
27. Finances	Needs met only through available funds	Pray, discern needs, present to people, press on in faith, praise Him for the provision (Phil. 4:14–19)
28. Attitudes	Conditional acceptance (James 2:1–4)	Unconditional acceptance (Rom. 15:7)
29. Ultimate concern	The church's reputation	Exalting Christ (Col. 1:18)
30. Result	A church that has a reputation for being alive but is really dead (Rev 3:1)	God is glorified (1 Cor. 10:31); people function as He intends (Eph. 4:11–16); the lost are reached (Mark 16:15)

I am indebted to Marlin "Butch" Hardman for the original concepts in this comparative chart.

Continuing the Quest to be a Spiritual Pioneer!

To continue your quest to find out more about what it means to be a Spiritual Pioneer and be a part of Authentic New Testament Christianity, please check out the following resources:

A New Testament Church in the Metro-Atlanta area dedicated to "becoming a people of His presence to IMPACT the world".
Larry Tomczak, Senior Pastor

www.ctkatlanta.com

"Show Your Glory": Original Praise & Worship from Worship Leader Matt Tommey & the Christ the King Worship Team.
Other worship resources also available from...

www.rainandfire.org

If you enjoyed *Reckless Abandon*, **here are some other titles from Charisma House that we think will minister to you...**

Follow the Fire
Steve Gray
ISBN: 0-88419-785-9
Retail Price: $13.99

Discover the consuming passion of God's love for you. Author Steve Gray draws from his experiences in the Smithton Outpouring revival to share with you the precious truths and kingdom insights that will help you enter a new level of intimacy with an awesome God.

The Missions Addiction
David Shibley
ISBN: 0-88419-772-7
Retail Price: $13.99

In these action-packed pages, you will discover a Global Jesus Generation that is creating discomfort in the church and change in missions worldwide. God is calling you to become part of a contagious epidemic of missions-hearted believers who will bring global fame to His name!

Nevertheless
Mark Rutland
ISBN: 0-88419-847-2
Retail Price: $9.99

With one unassuming word, Jesus freed us and revealed the love of God. Jesus captured the awesome power of this word in the Garden of Gethsemane. Jesus prayed, and heaven and earth rejoiced. If you want to confuse the enemy—say *Nevertheless*. Should terrible events threaten to overwhelm you and rip at the foundations of your soul, remember you still have an answer...*Nevertheless*.

Charisma®
HOUSE

To pick up a copy of any of these titles, contact your local Christian bookstore or order online at www.charismawarehouse.com.

Your Walk With God Can Be Even Deeper...

With *Charisma* magazine, you'll be informed and inspired by the features and stories about what the Holy Spirit is doing in the lives of believers today.

Each issue:
- Brings you exclusive world-wide reports to rejoice over.
- Keeps you informed on the latest news from a Christian perspective.
- Includes miracle-filled testimonies to build your faith.
- Gives you access to relevant teaching and exhortation from the most respected Christian leaders of our day.

Call 1-800-829-3346 for 3 FREE trial issues
Offer #A2CCHB

If you like what you see, then pay the invoice of $22.97 (**saving over 51% off the cover price**) and receive 9 more issues (12 in all). Otherwise, write "cancel" on the invoice, return it, and owe nothing.

Experience the Power of Spirit-Led Living

Charisma Offer #A2CCHB
P.O. Box 420234
Palm Coast, Florida 32142-0234
www.charismamag.com

1884A